'Jesus was loved by the poo  in our day the church is st struggling in areas of depr His head! The reason th challenging is that it tells th who secured a huge following or thousands of working class men". How did he do it? Read this relevant book to find the answer.'
Rt Rev James Jones KBE, the former Bishop of Liverpool

'As a leader in the Baptist community of Merseyside and the North-west it is truly humbling to realise how much of what we have inherited today owes its origins to the endeavour and commitment of one man and those he inspired and gathered around him.

'This is a story of unstinting commitment to making the message of Christ, in its every expression, accessible to everyone; a calling that was fuelled by a deep personal commitment to live as a follower of Jesus in every circumstance. We owe a debt to Wayne Clarke for bringing this story to the attention of a new generation, and we owe this story a resolve to reclaim and nurture that same spirit of gospel commitment and missional enterprise that Hugh Stowell Brown and his contemporaries so took for granted.'
Rev Phil Jump, Regional Minister for the North Western Baptist Association

'Wayne Clarke has placed us all in his debt by this account of the life, ministry, theology and social engagement of Hugh Stowell Brown, a leading Baptist minister, a man of great influence in Liverpool and an original thinker and activist within the Dissenting communities, especially in the north west of England and in Scotland.

'Mr Clarke explores the early life of Manxman Hugh Stowell Brown growing up in an impoverished home in the Isle of Man, one of the children of a poorly paid Church of England parson. His conversion to Baptist views as a young man working in the Midlands led him to a lifetime of service at Myrtle Street Baptist Chapel in Liverpool, where he drew thousands to hear him.

'The life of Hugh Stowell Brown demonstrates the breadth of this key Victorian preacher. He could draw a crowd of thousands to his Sunday afternoon open-air preaching; his ability to speak on topics he had researched thoroughly was noted not only in Liverpool, but also throughout the country. During his year of Presidency of the Baptist Union (1878–1879) he had important things to say about theological education by apprenticeship. He was concerned for social change, supporting C H Spurgeon in the development of the Stockwell Orphanage and founding a bank for working people in Liverpool.

'This dynamic account is an important contemporary addition to our knowledge of an outstanding Baptist minister in the north, which deserves careful study.'

Rev Dr Keith G Jones, President of the Baptist Historical Society

A READY MAN

Hugh Stowell Brown
Preacher, activist, friend of the poor

WAYNE CLARKE

instant
apostle

First published in Great Britain in 2019

Instant Apostle
The Barn
1 Watford House Lane
Watford
Herts
WD17 1BJ

British Library Cataloguing-in-Publication Data

A catalogue record for this book is available from the British Library.

This book and all other Instant Apostle books are available from Instant Apostle:

Website: www.instantapostle.com

E-mail: info@instantapostle.com

ISBN 978-1-912726-08-0

Printed in Great Britain.

Contents

Acknowledgements

This short work has taken some years to research and write, alongside the work of a busy Baptist minister. But as with most things in life, it has only come about through partnership and cooperation with many good people along the way.

Much of the work on this book was done during two periods of sabbatical study leave. My first sabbatical was from Dovedale Baptist Church in Liverpool, whose history inspired my interest in Hugh Stowell Brown. My second sabbatical was from New North Road Baptist Church, Huddersfield. I am grateful to these churches for allowing me to take time to give to this and to other projects. I am also grateful for the love and prayers of my current church, Trinity Baptist Church, Gorton, Manchester.

During my first sabbatical I drew on the resources of the Liverpool Library Archive and Family History Collection, which holds the records of Myrtle Street Baptist Church, including minute-books from church meetings and deacons' meetings. During my second sabbatical I spent some days studying at the Angus Library at Regent's Park College in Oxford and at the library of the IBTS in Amsterdam, which both hold invaluable resources in Baptist history. I am grateful to staff at these institutions for their support.

With regard to the statue, I was helped enormously by Nick Roberson of Roberson Stonecarving, by whose hands the Hugh Stowell Brown statue was restored. Nick made a generous and most helpful contribution to the chapter on the statue and I owe him a large debt of gratitude, as we all do for his skilful restoration work.

I would also thank Rev Dr David Steers for allowing the use of his excellent photographs from his velvethummingbee blog,[1] and Bryan Dunleavy, whose excellent Wolverton Past blog[2] gives context to the years Brown spent working in Wolverton. Far and away the most useful resource for the history of the Isle of Man to support my research on Brown's early life is Francis Coakley's *A Manx Notebook*, which is available online at http://www.isle-of-man.com/manxnotebook.

Remarks attributed to Hugh Stowell Brown in this account, if not otherwise attributed, are to be found in *Hugh Stowell Brown, A Memorial Volume*, published in 1888, after his death, by George Routledge and Sons, and edited by his son-in-law W S Caine MP. This volume can be found in two versions: one that includes extracts from his sermons and some articles by his friends, and one slimmer volume of just his memoirs and his *Commonplace Book*. The memoirs, though not the *Commonplace Book*, can be found reproduced online as part of 'A Manx Notebook' at this website: http://www.isle-of-man.com/manxnotebook/fulltext/hsb1888/index.htm.

Brown wrote his memoirs (*Notes of My Life*) and his notebook, without ever intending them to be published. In editing Brown's notebooks, Caine removed some

---

[1] https://velvethummingbee.wordpress.com.

[2] http://wolvertonpast.blogspot.com.

unfavourable material and redacted some names and admits that he added 'a few pages' of his own, but this remains the most trustworthy original source material we have for Hugh Stowell Brown's life.

Although other people have given much in time, wisdom and information, all errors and mistakes in this work remain mine and I would be grateful for discussion and correction of any matters mentioned here through social media or at my website, www.wayneclarke.org. At this site the reader will also find more information on Hugh Stowell Brown and a number of photographs.

I offer continuing thanks to my wife, Val Clarke, for her loving support and to our Lord Jesus Christ, in whom 'we live and move and have our being' (Acts 17:28, NIV).

This work is dedicated to the members of Dovedale Baptist Church, Liverpool, who faithfully continued the work of Hugh Stowell Brown in the city he loved, and to the glory of God.

Introduction

A statue in Hope Street, Liverpool, depicts a bearded Victorian gentleman holding a notebook and a penny. He is sculpted in marble and stands above street level on a large plinth. The statue itself has a fascinating history. Its creation through public subscriptions is testimony to the reputation of the man it commemorates. It was saved from the attacks of misguided vandalism. For a long time the statue lay lost and abandoned, neglected and open to erosion in a council farmyard. Its restoration very close to the place where it originally stood is a remarkable achievement.

The statue is to Hugh Stowell Brown, a largely forgotten hero of Victorian Liverpool. Brown came to Liverpool from the Isle of Man in his early twenties and gave the rest of his life to the town. He led a church, Myrtle Street Baptist Church, which welcomed rich and poor, and spread its influence across a wide region of the country. He worked among the poor of the town, concerned for their housing needs and their social environment as well as their spiritual well-being. He had a heart for the seafarers and for the many widows they left behind.

Hugh Stowell Brown was also a formidable teacher, preacher and lecturer. He was a man of learning with a common touch, a friend of the poor, who could combine biblical wisdom with common-sense advice of how to navigate a course through life in a changing world.

It is hoped that this short introduction to the life of Hugh Stowell Brown will allow those who see the statue on Hope Street to get to know a little of the man himself, of the times he lived in and of what he stood for.

1
His Early Days

The weather was typically stormy in the tempestuous channel between the Isle of Man and Great Britain on the night of 19th November 1830. The cruel winds drove the steam packet *St George* on to St Mary's Rock in Douglas Bay. The wrecking of the steamship was one of Hugh Stowell Brown's earliest memories. The entire crew was rescued and not a life was lost, thanks to the efforts of the lifeboat crew under the command of Sir William Hillary. Hillary was sixty years old and he nearly lost his life in the daring rescue that day. A commemorative plaque in Douglas Bay reads:

> Sir William, accompanied by Lieut. Robinson, Capt. Corlett, and fourteen volunteer boatmen, with the veteran coxswain Isaac Vondy, rescued all on board consisting of twenty-two persons. Sir William was washed overboard against the wreck, and was with difficulty saved, having had six ribs fractured and was otherwise much hurt.

The wreck of the *St George* led to the building of the Tower of Refuge on Conister Rock, and it pushed forward plans that Sir William Hillary had for a national fleet of lifeboats that became the Royal National Lifeboat Institution.

Storms at sea became a driving force for significant changes in the early life of Hugh Stowell Brown. A hurricane of 1839 presaged his initial move away from the island of his birth to England and his working life. And it was because of another stormy night in the winter of late 1846 that his father died, and his hopes for training for Baptist ministry were torn away from him.

Memorial to William Hillary in Douglas Bay (photo: Wayne Clarke)

The year of his birth

There is no record of the weather conditions on the day Hugh Stowell Brown was born, Sunday 10th August 1823, in Douglas, the principal town of the Isle of Man. Douglas was the largest town and port on the Island, though not then the capital of the Island, which was Castletown, ten miles to the south-west. Douglas was the only port allowed by law to receive wine and spirits and international produce and so was a busy place of trade and had a population of 6,000.

Pigot's Directory, a commercial directory and guide to the town, describes Douglas in the year that Brown was born:

> The streets are for the most part singularly irregular, crooked, and narrow, though they contain many excellent houses and inns. The general shape of the town is triangular, and, in this respect, it has been compared to the Manks Arms, which are three legs.[3]

The grandest church in Douglas was St George's, built in 1761 on the edge of the town, but the central church was still St Matthew's, built in the heart of the town in 1708. This was the church where Hugh's father, the Rev Robert Brown, was minister, known as the chaplain. The church was not large, and seated 360 people. A history of the church describes its interior:

> The high-backed pews with their locked doors ... the yellow-washed walls, the rotting floors, the lofty forbidding altar rail, with the three-decker pulpit in front obscuring the altar, the low gallery at the west end supported by pillars, combined to form a very plain and uninspiring interior.[4]

---

[3] *Pigot's Isle of Man Directory and Guide,* 1823, included in the *New Commercial Directory of Scotland* (Pigot & Co., 1825).

[4] Hugh Selwyn Taggart, MA, vicar, *The Story of S. Matthew's Church, Douglas Isle of Man* (Douglas: S H Broadbent & Co Ltd Printers, c 1923).

St Matthew's was described in *Johnson's Guide* of 1850 as:

> an old and ungainly edifice ... it affords but slender accommodation, and stands in a very inconvenient situation, being almost in the centre of the only open space in Douglas.[5]

Inconvenient though it may have been to the town's development, St Matthew's was literally a church in the Market Place, at the heart of the life of the commercial centre of the Island. The old St Matthew's eventually proved too much of an inconvenience for the commercial development of the town and was demolished in 1898 to allow for the development of the Market Square. It was replaced by the new St Matthew's at the North Quay.

As well as the two parish churches, part of the Church of England's Diocese of Sodor and Man, there was a Catholic church some distance out of the town, and a thriving community of over 1,000 Wesleyan Methodists. The Primitive Methodists began a mission in the town in 1823, and there was an Independent chapel in Athol Street, where later Hugh was an occasional preacher.

A third parish church, St Barnabas, was built in 1830, and Brown records in his *Notes of My Life* the laying of the foundation stone of the new church, just 250 yards from St Matthew's, as one of his early memories. He says, 'My father never liked that enterprise. It threatened him with extinction, and I do not think it was at all necessary to build

[5] James Brotherston Laughton, BA, *Johnson's Historical, Topographical, & Parochial Illustrated Guide, and Visitor's Companion through the Isle of Mann*, sixth edition (Douglas: Samuel Johnson, Duke Street, 1850).

the new church so near the old.' A writer called Train in his history of the Isle of Man of 1845 saw the increasing number of churches as not being in competition with each other, but serving different communities. He writes:

It may be considered one of the peculiarities of Douglas, that the natives of every country have there the advantage of attending their own church and their own minister. The native Manks have their St. Matthew's or St. Maughold's, with a native pastor. The English have their church dedicated to St. George, with an English minister. The Scots have their kirk, with a clergyman connected with the presbytery of Lancashire; and the Irish have their St. Barnabas (it should have been St. Patrick); while the old ship is a common receptacle for the outcasts of all nations. In most of the parish churches throughout the Island, divine service is performed alternately in English and Manks.[6]

By the religious census of the Island of 1851 the population of Douglas had grown to 9,980, of whom only 385 were worshippers at St Matthew's, while St George's and the new St Barnabas each had more than 1,300. At this time the best attended church in the town was the Factory Lane Primitive Methodist Chapel which had over 1,600 people, and the number of Methodists overall nearly equalled the Anglican total.

Pigot's Directory for 1823 describes the qualities of Douglas in glowing terms. It speaks of the 'national free

---

[6] Joseph Train, *Historical and Statistical Account of the Isle of Man* (Douglas, Isle of Man, 1845).

school' with a school roll of over 300 children, and of 'numerous' private seminaries. It speaks of the town's stone pier as its 'most prominent feature', calling it a 'great beauty and attraction' and 'the resort of all the beauty and fashion of the place'. The *Directory*, clearly wanting to attract business to the town, also waxes eloquently on the inns, public libraries, newsrooms, billiard rooms and even 'dancing assemblies and card assemblies' in the town.

The *Directory* goes on to list the 'nobility, gentry and clergy' of the town including the Rev Robert Brown, described as 'Master of the Douglas Grammar School, Chapel Street'. In *Notes of My Life*, Hugh Stowell Brown recalls some of the people he knew in his early years in Douglas. He recalls the paucity and slow progress of the steamers to Liverpool, and the transport round the Island as being poor and perilous. He recounts how the journey to Peel or Castletown or Ramsey was a very slow one in a carrier's cart which 'stopped at every public-house upon the road'. As there was a pub for every mile that meant that the carrier and the passengers would complete their journeys very much the worse for drink.

An Island heritage

Young Hugh's world was a small one and most of the people living in Douglas were of Manx descent with Manx names such as Caine, Cannell, Clague, Clucas, Corlett, Corren, Cosnahan, Kelly, Quane and Quirk. Hugh dismissively describes the Manxmen as 'not remarkable either for temperance, diligence or cleanliness. They were in those days chiefly small farmers, whose land was most wretchedly neglected and whose houses and homesteads were utter horrors of discomfort, disorder and filth.'

The Tower of Refuge, Douglas Bay, Isle of Man (photo: Wayne Clarke)

One of the best-known landmarks in Douglas is the 'Tower of Refuge' on Conister Rocks. This was completed in 1832, and built as a direct response to the wrecking of the *St George* in 1830. Hugh's memories of Douglas Bay in his memoirs are from the time after the sinking of the *St George* and before the Tower's completion. He writes of happy times playing among the rocks. He says:

> The baths, the shipyard, the shore, were our playground. We also frequented the harbour, with its quay and pier stretching out into the bay ... There was no Tower of Refuge of Conister Rock; I just remember the wreck of a steamer called 'St George'.[7]

[7] Hugh Stowell Brown, ed W S Caine, *Notes of My Life,* in *Hugh Stowell Brown, A Memorial Volume* (London: George Routledge and Sons 1888), p 7.

Hugh Stowell Brown's family line has been traced back to the early seventeenth century. Their seagoing heritage can be traced to a Captain Robert Brown, born in 1713 to John Brown and Alice Stole (or Stowell) of Ballastole in the north-east of the Island. The Stowell family line derives from Somerset from before the Norman Conquest. Captain Robert Brown made his living at sea as the owner and master of a Douglas trading ship.

Captain Robert married Margaret Cosnahan and their eighth child was also called Robert, and followed his father's occupation, becoming a sea captain. This Robert was born in 1761, the same year that St George's Church was opened. The Island at this time was clearly short of surnames, because Robert's sister Ann married another member of the Stowell clan, a Thomas Stowell. Ann became the mother to fifteen sons and one daughter, including the Hugh Stowell who later gave his name to his cousin Hugh Stowell Brown.

On 24th October 1784 Robert married Jane Drumgold, herself the daughter of a Stowell, and they had two sons. The first died in infancy and the second, another Robert, was Hugh Stowell Brown's father. Captain Robert Brown, Hugh's grandfather, is recorded as being captain of the brig Caesar in 1775 and 1782. He died at sea in 1800 when his son was only eight years old.

Rev Robert Brown, Hugh's father, was born in Douglas in 1792 and was the most influential person in Hugh's life. From an early age he was studious and always loved church history and classics. He was known as a faithful pastor and a passionate preacher, always preaching his sermons without notes because of his poor eyesight. His voice is recorded as being 'musical, delicate and vibrant'. He preached an evangelical message, very 'Low Church' and biblical. He was also known as a composer of hymn tunes and he published a volume of poetry in 1826.

Hugh Stowell Brown's mother was Agnes Dorothy Thompson, known as Dorothy. She and Robert were married at Kirk Braddan on 21st April 1819. Dorothy was born on the Island of a Scottish father, John Thompson of Jedburgh. Dorothy's mother was Eleanor Birkett, probably the daughter of Rev Thomas Birkett, a Cumbrian man who had been vicar at St Matthew's until 1735.

The young family

Robert and Dorothy had ten children from 1820 to 1839. The eldest was, of course, called Robert, and then came John, who died at the age of two, just after the birth of the third, named Hugh Stowell after his father's cousin, by then the vicar of Lonan on the Island and soon to be rector of Balaugh. Hugh Stowell was an evangelical activist who established the first Sunday school on the Island and was a well-known author and biographer who had also edited the Manx New Testament of 1810.

Hugh's younger brother by seven years was Thomas Edward Brown. T E Brown is still widely remembered in the Isle of Man for his writing. There is a statue of him in Douglas town centre and he is known as the national poet of the Isle of Man. Tom, as Hugh always called him, was the brother who most closely matched Hugh in intellect and faith, but, being the younger brother, did not have the family responsibilities that fell to Hugh. Tom studied at

Christ Church, Oxford, and obtained a fellowship at Oriel College. He became a teacher and lived most of his life in Bristol where he was headmaster of Clifton College. From the 1880s he published poetry in the Manx dialect of English and was heralded on his death in 1897 as the greatest Manx poet.

Old Kirk Braddan (photo: Wayne Clarke)

Although Tom and Hugh saw little of each other in later life, it is clear from Tom's letters that his relationship with his older brother was very significant to him. One of T E Brown's best-known narrative poems, published in his *Fo'c's'le Yarns* (1881), is called 'Captain Tom and Captain Hugh', a poetic tale of two sea captains who are best friends. It is a poem about brotherhood, but also about conflict and loss. In a letter of 1886 Tom wrote, 'My brother has ringed me around all my life with moral strength and abettance.'[8] A friend, E M Oakeley, recalled Thomas' words:

[8] Sidney T Irwin (ed), *Letters of Thomas Edward Brown, Author of Fo'c'sle Yarns* (Westminster, Archibald Constable and Co, 1900), p 118.

there are people to whom to coexist is life: no need to see them or talk to them. All that is needed is just to think – say in your bath at 7am – 'Hugh also is'.[9]

Hugh was baptised into the Church of England privately and quietly soon after his birth, but there was no public ceremony, until what he calls his 'christening' after his brother Tom was born in 1830. In that year there was a great ceremony when not only Tom but Hugh, his brother William and sister Dora were all christened together. This separation of Christian baptism from a public ceremony was a sign of Robert's uncertainty about infant baptism, one his son was to share, and which would cause him later to leave the Church of England. Hugh reflects that at the end of the public christening of the four children, his father would have 'laughed at the whole business as a piece of humbug'. Robert was, according to Hugh 'one of the lowest of the Low Churchmen, who would take such liberties with the rules as would make most Low Churchman of these days stand aghast'. Robert's services omitted the reading of the creed, ignored the lectionary set for each service and had no time for saints' days or even the routines of Holy Week.

The biggest change in Hugh's early life was the move from Douglas to Kirk Braddan. From being a teacher and vicar of the town-centre church, Robert moved to be the curate of Kirk Braddan, just outside the town of Douglas, but seen as a 'country parish'. Robert was to be the curate in name, but in reality he ran the parish, when Rev Thomas Howard moved into town to be vicar at St George's and

---

[9] Irwin (ed), *Letters of Thomas Edward Brown,* p 44.

officially retained the 'living' at Braddan. So in November 1832, when Hugh was nine, the family moved two and a half miles into a country vicarage surrounded by fields and farms, with a view over Douglas and the Irish Sea, and the coast of Cumberland visible beyond. For Hugh and for his brothers Robert, twelve, and William, seven, it was wonderful and exciting to live in the countryside. For their mother, now having three other children under five and with three more to follow soon, it was perhaps not so appealing. The vicarage was small with low ceilings, and had only two proper bedrooms apart from Robert's study and a dark attic room, which both had to be used for sleeping accommodations as more children arrived.

Kirk Braddan, now known as Old Kirk Braddan, felt old and crumbling when the Browns moved there in 1832. It had been rebuilt in 1777 but had no 'mod cons'. The vestry was dark, damp and unusable, with no heating, no cushions, no organ and no choir. It had, and still has, forbidding and dark box pews and a gallery. It has a Georgian 'three-decker' pulpit, with a lectern where the parish clerk would sit, a second level from where the minister would conduct the service and a higher pulpit above for delivering the sermon. Robert Brown's congregation did not join in either responses or hymns but, as Hugh puts it, 'sat and knelt and stood absolutely mute'.

There were two new challenges for the curate of Kirk Braddan: preaching in Manx and taking funerals. It was expected that sermons should be given alternately in English and in Manx, which Robert Brown didn't speak at all. So he learned this new language and set about the duty of delivering sermons in a language that no more than a dozen people in the parish spoke better than English. Brown's incumbency, which began officially in 1836, was a time of change for the church. Its first organ was installed in 1837, and in 1839 the building was upgraded with new limestone flooring. But despite moving with the times, the church stopped being the parish church in 1876 when the new Kirk Braddan was consecrated.

Funerals were a burden because no other parish church in Douglas had a graveyard, so every Sunday afternoon there was a funeral, sometimes five at a time. This was multiplied many times over during the cholera outbreak of 1833, though for Hugh and his brothers it was more remembered for the five months without having to go to school rather than the dreadful consequences in the loss of life. Later in life Hugh considered the Manx people's attitude to the cholera outbreak as typifying their superstitious outlook on life – that instead of clearing their houses, streets and harbours of filth and rotten fish, and drinking less rum, they turned to prayer. For Hugh, faith was always to walk hand-in-hand with good practical common sense, and never to be a retreat from it.

Old Kirk Braddan interior (photo: Wayne Clarke)

School life

The schooling that Hugh and his brothers eventually began was very poorly delivered and ineffectual. Their school was the house that the Browns had recently left in Chapel Street in Douglas, so going to school meant going back to Hugh's previous home. Douglas Grammar School had only two teachers. The senior master was the man who had taken over from Rev Robert Brown as chaplain at St Matthew's. He was Rev John Stowell, a distant relative, and he was assisted by his uncle, William Stowell. John Stowell was a Manxman who had been to Oxford, and within a year he was appointed vice-principal of the prestigious King William's College, a public school which was just opening in Castletown. Hugh had a very low opinion of John Stowell whose Latin was poor and Greek non-existent but remembered him as 'well-armed; he carried a cane. The cane was used without the slightest regard to justice or to mercy.' Hugh considered John Stowell's appointment to King William's College to be a political one after the trustees had appointed an Englishman to be principal of a college that was meant to educate the cream of Manx society. His departure was only a temporary cause for rejoicing however as his successor was, according to Hugh, 'of all men who ever undertook to keep a school, the greatest duffer'.

The older teacher, William Stowell, had a more permanent influence on Hugh. Although he was a poor teacher, he was more merciful in his punishment. He had lived most of his life in Liverpool as a ship painter and came under the influence of Dr Raffles at Great George Street Chapel, a leading Independent church in the town.

He was the first person Hugh had met who had left the Church of England for reason of conscience, which Hugh regarded as a courageous act. William Stowell was a member of the Independent Church in Douglas, where a few years later Hugh first tried his hand at preaching and had his first sense of calling to the ministry that would become his life blood. Hugh recalls one incident that began his journey to becoming a 'Dissenter'. School on a Saturday was the day the boys were taught the catechism of the Anglican Church. But the teachers who were also church ministers were preparing their sermons that day, so the duty to teach the catechism fell to William Stowell. Stowell only taught the boys the sections of the catechism that he believed, including the Lord's Prayer and the Ten Commandments, but not the parts that referred to baptism or the sacraments, which he regarded as superstitious. Later, Hugh's reflection on the parts of the catechism that William had taught and those he had omitted was a major factor in his move away from the established Church.

At school Hugh took his young brother Tom under his wing. Compared with the studious Thomas, Hugh was described as being full of 'daring and vigour', and while Tom delighted in learning Latin, Hugh had a more natural inclination towards science and mechanics. It is recorded by his brother Tom that while he was still at school Hugh built his first steam engine and already intended to be an engineer.

Douglas Grammar School only had lessons in the mornings. Six mornings a week the Brown boys, Robert, Hugh and Will and then Tom and Harry went off to school, while Dora stayed at home with their mother, joined in time by Margaret, Harriet and baby Alfred. Hugh's early promise had earned his family a grant from the Murray Foundation, which gave grants to young men being prepared from an early age for the ministry of the Church. The Foundation paid Hugh's fees at Douglas Grammar School and £5 a year in addition, though Hugh saw very little of this himself.

Each afternoon their father was supposed to give the boys their lessons. Robert's eyesight was getting worse and by the time Hugh was eleven years old his father could no longer read without pain. Instead of offering formal lessons Robert called on his son Hugh to read for him every afternoon and every evening. For four years Hugh would watch his brothers playing on the hills outside while he stayed in to read to his father.

While Robert puffed on his pipe, a habit his son would soon learn to imitate, Hugh read to him for four or five hours at a stretch. This reading Hugh described as 'my best school'. The regular practice of reading out loud was excellent preparation for a life of preaching, lecturing and speaking to large crowds out of doors. The material he read trained his mind and gave him a broad base of knowledge that served him well all his life. He read Virgil, Horace, Ovid and Cicero in Latin. He read theology and biblical commentary from Baxter to Paley to Matthew Henry. History was provided by Gibbon, Hume and others, and poetry by Shakespeare, Milton, Dryden and Pope. There was also lighter reading: *The Spectator*, *The Rambler* and the *Morning Herald*.

By the time he was fifteen, Hugh was better read than any young man of his age and felt ready to leave home.

Despite the Foundation money, Hugh decided not to follow his father into Christian ministry, but he was set on seeing the world. His brother Robert had already joined a merchant ship and left home; now it was Hugh's turn to see what there was of the world beyond the Isle of Man.

2
The Working Man

A hurricane which hit the Isle of Man on the 6th and 7th January 1839 was blowing a wind of change for the fifteen-year-old Hugh Stowell Brown. There was a world to see and a world of work to enter. His opportunity to learn a trade came from a friend of the family, an old Scottish doctor on the Island, Dr MacFarlane, whose son David was working in England for the Tithe Commutation Survey and looking for an apprentice.

For Hugh's mother, Dorothy, it must have been painful to watch her third son, Hugh, leave home on 19th February 1839. Although the eldest, Robert, had already flown the nest, Hugh was the one she had always assumed would follow his father into Christian ministry. With six young children to look after, the normal anxiety of a son leaving home must have been increased for Dorothy by the loss of the one who carried many of her greatest hopes.

Hugh's new job was in Biddulph in Staffordshire and the first leg of his journey was a rough crossing to Liverpool on the *King Orry* steamer, a ten-hour voyage in what Hugh called 'an awful old tub'. This was Hugh's second visit to Liverpool, having previously made the journey to visit his brother. The town that was to be his home eight years later was for the fifteen-year-old just a place to change modes of transport and take his first-ever journey by train. His point of embarkation was the newly opened Lime Street station and as he approached the station he would have passed by Lime Street chapel. This chapel, under the ministry of James Lister, was a rapidly growing town-centre church, which just two years later was bought up by the Liverpool Corporation to redevelop the railway station. The church was to move to Myrtle Street, in which location Brown would succeed James Lister as the church's pastor.

But at 9 am that Wednesday morning the young man setting out into the world was not concerned for chapels, but for booking a place for his first train journey. He records how in those days it was literally a 'booking' as, when you gave your name, it was written in a big book and you received your ticket which bore the number of your carriage and your seat. He recalls with some embarrassment that he spent more than he might have done on the ticket: 'Young fool that I was, I must needs have first-class.' However, the second-class carriages in those days were very much open to the elements, with no sides, but just a rough roof for shelter. The train left the wooden sheds of the railway station, through a dark tunnel emerging into Olive Mount cutting, and on to the industrial sites and mills of Warrington, two hours later arriving at the railway centre of Crewe.

Off to Biddle

Hugh's new job was with a land surveyor for the Tithe Commutation Survey. In 1836 parliament had passed the Tithe Commutation Act. This brought an end to the ancient system of local taxes in which people paid a tithe or a tenth of their crops or produce to the rector of a parish or to a private landlord, who stored up the tithe in local tithe barns. By the 1830s this system was outdated and the cause of discontent. Under the new system tithes could be made in monetary value, known as the corn rent. This new system was welcomed by Catholics and by nonconformists who did not wish to pay taxes to the Church of England. In order to introduce the new system, areas affected by the act had to be surveyed and maps had to be drawn up, known as tithe maps. From 1836 to 1841 there was a rush of land surveying and map-making, which then led to the 1841 Ordnance Survey Act, which gave surveyors the right of entry to properties, and led to the complete mapping of Britain.

For four months Hugh worked with David MacFarlane on the survey of Biddulph. To get there he first had to go by coach from Crewe to Congleton, where he contrived to spend the night at the wrong hostelry and then had to walk to next day to Biddulph, or 'Biddle' as Hugh soon learned it was known to the locals. He writes of how he was directed there: 'Happen it's Biddle you want; yes, that is t' reet ro-ad, and when you coom to t' next housen, you mun turn to t' reet, and t' place is nelly two moile further on.'[10] By these directions he found his way to Whitmore Cottage in Biddulph and found the two surveyors, MacFarlane and Robert Wyatt.

The work of a land surveyor involved a lot of walking and carrying heavy equipment. The basic tool of the trade

[10] Hugh Stowell Brown, ed W S Caine, *Notes of My Life*, in *Hugh Stowell Brown, A Memorial Volume*, p 29.

was the chain – a metal chain sixty-six feet long with a handle at each end. The 'chain' became an accepted unit of length, still seen to this day in use in the railways. Its legacy survives in the length of a cricket pitch, which is one chain between the stumps. The job of the junior surveyor or 'chainman' was to hold on to one end of the chain and to throw the other end forward where it was stretched out and marked by the senior surveyor, the 'rodman'. Hugh called the work 'healthy to mind and body', but it involved a lot of physical exertion, including clambering over walls and through hedges and across streams. Hugh also considered the work a good exercise for his preaching voice as most conversations were held a chain's length apart.

Hugh had to grow up quickly during his four months in Biddulph. The area they were surveying included the hill of Mow Cop and the wilds of Biddulph Moor where Hugh met a group of people who were locally reputed to be of a Moorish race, and according to legend were descendants from a group of Saracen warriors captured during the Crusades. His time in Biddulph was also the first time he encountered a culture of smoking and drinking. MacFarlane and Wyatt were both heavy drinkers and Hugh was included in their regular drinking bouts. On his first full day of employment the working day ended in the Black Lion. Hugh had never before smoked a pipe and only ever tasted ale a few times, but here he was included in the smoking and drinking and ended up falling into a ditch on the walk home. It was the first and only time he was ever to get drunk, but it gave him an awareness of the effects of too much strong drink and enabled him later in life to speak about drunkenness from some personal experience. One part of his life that didn't change in the months in Biddulph was churchgoing. Each Sunday evening he went to church, usually at the parish church in Congleton with MacFarlane and Wyatt.

By June the survey work in Biddulph was completed and Hugh returned home, still not yet sixteen but feeling very much more grown-up, and much more awkward among his family. In November the last of his siblings, Alfred, was born, and with seven children now at home, including three under the age of five, the little house in Braddan felt very crowded. So when David MacFarlane contacted him to offer him more work in Shrewsbury, Hugh readily went back to surveying.

Shrewsbury and beyond

Shrewsbury was reached by steamer to Liverpool, ferry to Birkenhead and then a cold and rough road journey by coach. The survey this time was of the parish of Condover, a village south of Shrewsbury, which meant every day started and finished with a four-mile walk. Heavy drinking was once more part of the working life. This was normally at the village pub in Condover with its welcoming log fire, which meant that the walk back to Shrewsbury was never easy, and on one occasion MacFarlane fell into a ditch and Hugh couldn't move him, and had to spend the night with him at the side of the road. This incident was one that later led Hugh to become a total abstainer.

Church life in Shrewsbury offered nothing to please the eager young man, and he found each of the parish churches in the town and the local Independent chapel equally dull. His judgement on Shrewsbury was harsh. He wrote in 1879: 'I found Shrewsbury a very stupid place, and it is a very stupid place still.'

In January 1840 the work at Condover was finished and the itinerant life of a Tithe Commutation Surveyor moved on to Harborne, now a suburb of Birmingham, then a village three miles from the town. The journey from Shrewsbury to Birmingham introduced Hugh to another form of transport, the omnibus, which wended its way through Wellington, Wolverhampton and the Black Country on a freezing cold January day. MacFarlane's drunkenness was becoming more frequent, and he arrived at his new assignment the worse for drink.

Hugh was no more impressed by Birmingham than Shrewsbury. He commented on the forlorn appearance of the town's streets and the street corners, full of 'hundreds of dirty, ragged and half-starved workmen'. Neither was he impressed with the preaching of Birmingham's best-known nonconformist preacher, John Angell James, a man who had been called to be the minister of the Carrs Lane Congregational Chapel at the age of twenty, and by 1840 was aged fifty-five and was still highly regarded for his preaching, and for his book: *The Anxious Enquirer after Salvation Directed and Encouraged*. It was in 1840 that James attended the world's first International Anti-Slavery Convention. Hugh went to his church a couple of times but with the arrogance of youth dismissed his preaching as plain and unimpressive.

The work at Harborne turned out to be far more difficult than MacFarlane had thought. He believed it was to be an easy assignment, correcting the details of an older map. Because of this he had accepted the work at a low rate of pay per acre, but when he got there he found that Harborne and the neighbouring Smethwick had grown more than the Survey had realised, and instead of green fields there were miles of streets, forges, factories and glassworks. What was to be one month's work would take at least four. The consequence was not only the anger of MacFarlane but also a lack of funds to buy the food that a growing sixteen-year-old needed. The work of land surveying, so pleasant in the moorlands of Biddulph, was not so appealing in the industrial towns of the West Midlands. When the work was finally completed in May 1840 Hugh went back to Braddan again a little wiser and more world-weary. He never again worked with David MacFarlane.

One consequence of being in the industrial Midlands was the ambition for a new career. Hugh had seen heavy industry for the first time and he fancied the idea of becoming an engineer. Later that idea was to bear fruit, but there is a postscript to Hugh's time as a surveyor. Through another family friend an opportunity came Hugh's way to work for the Ordnance Survey in York. Hugh was to spend one more month in surveying and it began with the opportunity to see more of England with a train journey from Liverpool to Manchester and on to Littleborough near Rochdale, and then a coach to Leeds, a journey of nine hours. The next day entailed a rail journey from Leeds to York in a second-class carriage with no seats, what was known as a 'stand-up'.

Hugh's short stay in York again found him surrounded by hard-drinking men. His work was to survey the part of

York that included the Minster, and to avoid the traffic the work began at three in the morning. Hugh found satisfaction throughout his life in knowing that the measurements on the Ordnance Survey map of what he considered England's finest minster were made by his own hands.

Wolverton and the railways

In July 1840 Hugh returned home again and another friend on the Island gave him the contact he needed to enter into the engineering profession in the burgeoning railway industry. His new job was in the engine works in Wolverton, working for the London and Birmingham Railway. Railway pioneer Robert Stephenson had built the Liverpool to Manchester line some years earlier, but Hugh considered that line just the preparation for his greatest work, the line from Euston Station in London, through Rugby and Coventry and ending in Birmingham's Curzon Street station. The line opened in 1838, and in the same year the Wolverton locomotive workshop was established by the L&BR near the halfway point between London and Birmingham.

Wolverton is now part of Milton Keynes, but in 1840 it was a very poor canal village, a stopover on the Grand Union Canal: it only grew to be a town of any size with the coming of the railways. Each one of the twenty trains each day on the L&BR stopped at Wolverton for ten minutes for refreshments, so it became well known as the place for a pleasant if brief respite from travelling. When Hugh went to work there, there were no more than twenty houses for the workforce in Wolverton, and others lodged in the nearby villages, or in the towns of Stony Stratford and Newport Pagnell. These towns, described by Hugh as 'very dull, dead-alive places' had grown up as stopping places for the coach and horses en route to and from London, and so they were in decline as the railway traffic increased. The railway people were not liked in the towns, which blamed them for the loss of their business. Trains in 1840 were of little use to the working people. The fastest journey from London to Birmingham took five hours and cost thirty-two shillings each way first class or twenty-five shillings second class, well outside the means of an ordinary working family. Hugh was earning four shillings a week in his first year at Wolverton, and his father was only earning £200 a year as a country parson.

Hugh's work was alongside about 500 men from Lancashire, Yorkshire, Scotland and Ireland. Most of the company's locomotives were made at the Clarence Foundry in Love Lane in Liverpool, and the work at Wolverton was the maintenance and repair of the locomotives. All the engine parts had to be made on-site. Iron had to be forged by hand and shaped by sledgehammers wielded by skilled and strong men. Surfaces had to be smoothed to perfection with hand tools. Precision machinery was engineered by the skill of hand and eye, without any modern mechanical processes. Hugh himself learned the job slowly, usually working small pieces of metalwork on the hand lathe. He described himself as an 'indifferent workman' but developed a great respect for the skill of his colleagues and the hard, hot, heavy work going on around him.

For three years Hugh worked at the Wolverton railway works and his wages rose from four shillings a week to six shillings – still not enough to live on without some supplement to his income sent from his father. His daily routine six days a week began at half past five, with a mile's walk to work, where he cooked his own breakfast at a forge. Dinner was at one back in his lodgings in Old Wolverton, and the day ended at half past five. He made friends with three men who were, like him, keen to read books and improve their minds. The four shared lodgings and spent their evenings reading and talking. Hugh's main study at this time was in mathematics.

The Wolverton railway works are still active (photo: Wayne Clarke)

A test of faith

Although the four companions were not all committed Christians, all four decided together to become teetotallers. This was a decision which shaped the rest of Hugh's life as an abstinence campaigner and a 'Rechabite' – a member of a group founded in 1835 which promoted total abstinence from alcoholic drinks. The group was named after a biblical tribe who lived in tents outside the city and did not drink alcohol.[11] Hugh started attending temperance meetings where he made his first poor attempts at public speaking. He started up a Sunday school in a local temperance coffee house but did not enjoy his attempts to work with children.

In the three years at Wolverton Hugh's Christian faith was being tested and, like the iron he worked with, in its testing it was proved, forged and refined. Most of his workmates were hard-drinking and godless, and he records that of the 500 workmen he didn't know more than a dozen who went to church. But those who were people of faith impressed him. In the early days of his time at Wolverton he was engaged in conversation by a Cockney man called John Page who invited him to go with him to the Independent chapel in Stony Stratford. Hugh records that Page was a quiet man who mainly kept his faith to himself, but that single invitation encouraged Hugh to a regular pattern of churchgoing and kept him from bad company.

The local parish churches were not welcoming to working men. The clergy were mostly country parsons of

[11] See Jeremiah 35:1-11.

the old school who were more concerned with riding to hounds than conducting services. Hugh's regular place of worship was Stony Stratford church where he remembered the parson as a man of 'extreme stupidity and dullness' who seemed mostly concerned with an injustice done to him earlier in life which had left him in a debtors' prison. The vicar at the neighbouring parish of Old Wolverton was esteemed no more highly: Hugh dismissed him as a 'dismal fool' who seldom attempted to preach a sermon.

A number of visits out from Wolverton were influential on the young Hugh. One was a three-day visit to London towards Christmas in 1841. The other was a Sunday in the village of Olney, some ten miles north east of Wolverton. Hugh knew Olney as the place where John Newton, the former slave-trader and hymn-writer, and William Cowper the poet had lived and worked from 1764 to 1786. Hugh says he saw the tree called Cowper's Oak under which the poet sat to write, and met a man who had known William Cowper, who had left Olney some fifty-five years previously.

Hugh preached his first open-air 'sermon' on a weekend visit to Northampton. In the Market Square on a Sunday afternoon he heard a Mormon preacher, and with his friend he engaged the preacher in a public debate. Meeting and debating with Mormons was to follow him later in life both in Liverpool and Salt Lake City in 1872 where, by coincidence, he heard the same Mormon preacher he had heard in Northampton deliver very much the same sermon.

Stony Stratford Baptist Church, now Stony Stratford Community Church (photo: Wayne Clarke)

To Stony Stratford

Hugh sometimes walked considerable distances on a Sunday to try to find church which would encourage or nurture him. He tried a number of nonconformist chapels including two in Stony Stratford. The Independent chapel which he had attended with John Page was better than the parish churches of the district, but he was not impressed with the preaching of the minister. The one chapel where he found preaching that engaged him was Stony Stratford

Baptist Church where he found the minister, Mr E L Forster, to be a good preacher and a man whose abilities left a favourable mark on the young, and very choosy, worshipper.

Stony Stratford was a Baptist church with a very long history. It was founded in 1657 and had several notable ministers in its early years including the writer Benjamin Keach, who introduced hymn-singing to Baptist churches. By the early nineteenth century the church building had fallen into very poor repair, but it was rebuilt, and reopened on 30th July 1832. Forster began his ministry at Stony Stratford in 1836 and was minister there until 1865.

Forster became a friend and a mentor to Hugh and within a few years would be the man who changed the course of Hugh's life. Writing after Hugh's death, Forster recalled in a letter to *The Freeman* magazine how he first met Hugh Stowell Brown:

> During my pastorate of thirty years at Stony Stratford, Bucks, the Wolverton Works of the London and North-Western Railway Company were completed. On a summer's Sunday evening we used to have some forty or fifty of the Wolverton workmen come a distance of two miles to our place of worship. During Mr. Brown's apprenticeship as an engineer he occasionally, though the son of a clergyman, would accompany the others, and dare to enter a Dissenting place of worship. It was in this way that I became acquainted with him. He, with a number of others were accustomed to spend an hour

or two with me at my residence, when we discussed
a variety of subjects relating to heaven and earth.[12]

One other person in Wolverton was a major influence
on the young man: the Rev George Weight. Wolverton had
grown rapidly since the railways arrived in 1838, but the
L&BR at first had made no provision for families or for
worship. The company then opened a 'British School', an
elementary school supported by the British and Foreign
School Society on behalf of the nonconformist churches.
This was followed by plans to build a parish church, and
plans were drawn up for St George the Martyr's Church to
be erected in Wolverton, the first church in the world to be
built by a railway company. The L&BR contributed £1,000
towards the building and a further £1,000 was raised
through public subscription. The railway company
contributed £50 annually towards the incumbent's stipend,
with the rest paid by the diocese.

In the summer of 1841 Rev George Weight was sent to
the parish, where he held services in a chapel in the school
while the church was being built. Brown was present with
a good number of the railway workers when the first
service was held on 21st November 1841. Neither the
school chapel nor the church was ever well attended by
railwaymen, partly because the church clerk was a
'knobstick', a worker who refused to join the union, or a
'scab'.

George Weight was an evangelical and former
nonconformist and Hugh considered him to be a very good
preacher. Weight proved to be an important figure in

---

[12] *The Freeman,* 5th March 1886.

Wolverton's development. Apart from seeing the completion of the new church, which opened in 1844, and developing the congregation in a room of the new school building, he was also led the drive to establish a Mechanics' Institute, only the second establishment of its kind in the country.

Hugh had several conversations with George Weight about entering into the Christian ministry. This was clearly something that Hugh had been considering for some time, perhaps ever since he left home, and the idea had been growing in his imagination. Weight encouraged Hugh and offered to teach him Greek, which Hugh had never learned. Hugh bought a Greek grammar book and lexicon and a Greek New Testament, and started to spend most of his evenings in this new study, opening up the Bible in a way he had never done before. His work at this time was fitting tubes into the boilers of locomotive steam engines and, as very little work was being done, he wrote out his Greek exercises on the engine's firebox with a stick of chalk. From this point on it was not the steam engine but the study of the Bible that was to be Hugh's passion.

3
The Call to Ministry

When Hannah in the Old Testament called out to the Lord to give her a son, she readily dedicated his life to the Lord's service. Susanna Wesley, mother of John and Charles, is known as the 'Mother of Methodism' for her influence over her sons. In a similar way Dorothy Brown might be remembered as the person of greatest influence over her best-known sons, Hugh and Thomas. While his father, Robert, educated his third son Hugh in Latin, English literature and theology, it was his mother who prayed for him and always knew he was set apart for a preaching ministry.

When Hugh wrote home in late 1843 that he was giving up a second apprenticeship and leaving Wolverton, Robert took no comfort in Hugh's intention to enter the ministry of the Church. For Robert his calling to Christian ministry had led to disappointment and poverty. He was constantly battling with the theology of the established Church and constantly struggling to feed his family. Robert was never to know that Hugh would become a preacher and a reformer of national significance and end up earning £900 a year, more than four times his own income, and so become probably the best-paid nonconformist minister in Britain. Dorothy simply knew that her son has received his vocation, and left the rest to her God.

And so, at the beginning of 1844 Hugh left Wolverton and returned once more to Kirk Braddan. Hugh was now twenty years old. He had seen the bright lights of Liverpool, Manchester, York and London and must have assumed the rest of his life was mapped out. He would study at King William's College for ordination, then take up a parish on the Island, maybe returning to his childhood home in Douglas or even taking over the parish from his father who would be fifty-five by the time Hugh was ordained. But there were more than a few twists and turns in his story still to follow.

Hugh came home with mixed feelings. Now approaching full adulthood at the age of twenty-one he didn't want to be a further financial burden on his father. He felt the call to ministry was a real one, but never felt that he would be depriving God of his talents if he had stayed in engineering, or that God couldn't bring in His kingdom without the help of Hugh Stowell Brown. Many people in a similar situation, especially in his age, would have spoken of the deep love for souls that God put in their heart or the wonder of the consecration of the whole self to God. Hugh never considered Christian ministry in those terms. Hugh had discovered in himself a talent for learning and a love and skill at public speaking. He loved God and His Word and His people, but beyond that he was unsure of where his calling would lead. Although he had grown up in a vicarage, Hugh had no experience of Christian leadership and had never preached a sermon in a church.

One relief from Robert's financial concerns was that as a son of a Manx clergyman Hugh could receive his training at King William's College at no cost to the family. He might have started his studies in January, but part of the college had been burned down in a fire and there wasn't room for another student for ordination. Hugh would start at the college in August and spend seven months at home studying with his father. It was as if Hugh were eleven years old again, staying at home reading in Latin to his father and studying Greek alone with no support. It was seven months of misery for both son and father alike.

King William's College, Castletown (photo: Wayne Clarke)

Off to King Billy's

In August 1844 Hugh moved from Kirk Braddan to Castletown, lodging with a Mrs Kewley close to King William's College. King William's was not really where he wanted to be; having spent a few years in England the Island felt claustrophobic and he would much rather have been studying at Oxford or Cambridge. The college principal was Rev Robert Dixon, an earnest evangelical scholar, who taught Hugh the Greek classical writers and the Greek New Testament, plus some Hebrew. Hugh also continued his studies in Latin and in mathematics, though the curriculum did not seem to include any training in theology, nor in the practical work of being a clergyman.

It may have not been Oxford or Cambridge but life was good in Castletown for the young student, and he took part in the life of the town, mixing with soldiers from the local garrison and spending time with the local vicar. In 1845 he was present as the new lieutenant governor of the Isle of Man, David Hope, the Queen's representative on the Island, was installed at Castle Rushen in Castletown. Hugh was also able to earn some money teaching the sons of one of the college masters.

Then, once again, just as it seemed that Hugh had set his mind on his future calling and career, there was a twist in the tale. King William's College was a very Anglican institution, and training for 'holy orders' caused Hugh to reconsider his beliefs. Although Hugh had been brought up an Anglican, his experience of the Christian faith has been remarkably broad. His father was the lowest of Low Church Anglicans and through his acquaintance with Forster and the Baptists in Stony Stratford he had found good fellowship with Christians who rejected the established Church and many of its teachings. By the time he had been at King William's for a year and was only one year away from ordination, he started to question the route which he was following.

Hugh had objections to some of the ordinances of the Church of England. The Church's teaching on the baptism of infants was a stumbling block. The Church of England, in its Prayer Book, taught that the proper and normal entry into the Church was through the baptism of the young children of believing parents. Young children were thus included into the Church, and on some interpretations were in that way made 'regenerate'. This, for Hugh, was against the teaching of the Bible and stood in the way of proper preaching of conversion and forgiveness. He considered the Church's teaching on baptism as 'repulsive'. Neither did Hugh have any time for the practice of confirmation, when those who have been baptised affirm their baptism vows for themselves. Hugh's father had neither taught nor practised confirmation and Hugh himself had not been confirmed. But Hugh was a young man of conscience and he believed that becoming a minister of the Church involved an acceptance of the teachings of the Church. In this regard his father's behaviour was part of the problem. While Robert found he could be a minister of the Church while he rejected a lot of its teachings, Hugh felt this was not fair to the Church or to himself, and could not follow his father's example.

Hugh reflected later in life that if there had been at the time a liberal or 'Broad Church' movement in the Church of England, he might well have stayed within it. If he could have followed the example of those who later discovered 'plausible ways of making the Church rules and creeds seem anything you please', he might have found a spiritual home among such people. But at the time his conscience wouldn't allow such a flexible view of following the rites of the Church. As well as baptism and confirmation, Hugh was uncomfortable with the burial service, which routinely promised heavenly rewards even at the burial of avowed atheists, and the communion service.

Hugh also claimed to have problems with the Athanasian Creed, though it is not clear what these problems were. This historic creed of the Church has been used by Christian churches since the sixth century and is a formal statement of two Christian doctrines: the Trinity and the status of Jesus Christ. There is no question in Hugh's preaching that he had any doubts about the traditional statement of these two doctrines. In the Kirk Braddan, the church in which he grew up, the Lord's Prayer was displayed on the wall next to the Nicene Creed, and he never expressed any doubts about this shorter and more concise statement of faith.

Hugh may have been concerned about the boldness of the opening statement of the Athanasian Creed: 'Whosoever will be saved: before all things it is necessary that he hold the Catholick Faith. Which Faith except every one do keep whole and undefiled: without doubt he shall perish everlastingly.'[13] Similarly, he may have had doubts about asserting the final lines, 'And they that have done good shall go into life everlasting: and they that have done evil into everlasting fire. This is the Catholick Faith: which except a man believe faithfully, he cannot be saved.'[14] Hugh most probably had two objections to this. First of all, the Creed states that these are words that must be believed for salvation: Hugh would have held that faith comes from Christ alone, not from the assertion of a set of beliefs.

---

[13] Athanasian Creed, lines 1-2, *Book of Common Prayer* (Cambridge: Cambridge University Press, 1662).

[14] Athanasian Creed, lines 43-44, *Book of Common Prayer*, ibid.

Secondly Hugh might have already developed some unorthodox ideas about death and the afterlife. We know from Hugh's later teaching and preaching that he held a view of eternal punishment that is called 'conditional immortality', that is that eternal life is the reward for a life lived under the Lordship of Jesus, but eternal punishment is the extinction of the soul, not an eternity in hell.

As Hugh completed his studies and was being prepared for ordination in the summer of 1846 he shared his concerns with his father and with his bishop. Robert Brown heard of his son's convictions and, to Hugh's surprise, seemed pleased with the objections that Hugh has settled upon, presumably because he shared many of them himself. Robert recommended that Hugh should leave King William's College and consider becoming a nonconformist minister. Hugh still thought he might be able to be ordained and become his father's curate. Robert was by this time in very poor health and Hugh had started walking home to Kirk Braddan on Saturday evenings and spending Sundays helping his father conduct his services. Hugh's brother Tom had moved to Castletown and enrolled at King William's College himself and his brother Will had gone to sea. Perhaps supporting Robert as his curate was the answer, despite his discomfort with the Church.

But the bishop had other ideas. The Bishop of Sodor and Man was Thomas Vowler Short, a High Church classical scholar, Oxford-educated friend of William Gladstone and teacher of two leaders of the Anglo-Catholic 'Oxford Movement', Edward Pusey and John Henry Newman. Bishop Short was known for his intolerance of Dissenters.

His overriding concern was for education, and he saw in Hugh Stowell Brown the makings of an ideal 'schoolteacher parson' after his ordination, and even had a job lined up for him to teach the children of the mining community at the Foxdale Mines in the centre of the Island. Hugh had no interest in the role and the prospect of being sent to such a position made his mind up once and for all. He wrote to Bishop Short and to the archdeacon, to tell them that he no longer wanted to be considered for ordination and that the training he had received for the ministry of the Church had convinced him that he could not remain 'an honest member of its communion'. Both reacted angrily to the insolence of this free-thinking young man, but the decision was made, and Hugh left both the college and the Church of England in June 1846.

Castle Rushen, Castletown (photo: Wayne Clarke)

Becoming a Baptist

But once again Hugh was left with the question of what to do with his life. He had now explored three possible directions, and all three had led to a dead end. This third one was the hardest to deal with. Dorothy was left wondering why her hopes for her son had come to this abrupt stop just as he was about to enter into ordained ministry and fulfil what she had always seen as his destiny. Robert had never been sure about Hugh's path to Anglican ministry anyway, but must have seen in his son a desire to serve his Lord. And then there was the money. So often in the Brown household it came down to the pounds, shillings and pence. Hugh describes in dramatic terms his feelings at that time, resolving that he would 'die rather than impose upon my father's limited resources'. But he had only a little savings, and before his twenty-third birthday he had given up on two apprenticeships and two years of ministerial training.

His first thought was to go back to engineering. So he left home to 'make my way in the world as best I could'. He went to Liverpool and sought work in the engine shops and in the docks, but there was no work and despair set in. He even considered throwing himself in the dock in his hopelessness. But there was still hope, even if it amounted to no more than a little money in his pocket and his own health and strength. He headed for Crewe, where the London and North Western Railway were working, and was advised by friends there that there was work going in Manchester. There he found Alexander Youlen, an old friend from Wolverton, and stayed with him while he looked for work. But there was no work in Manchester, even with the Town Mission. Youlen had become a Baptist and in conversation with him and the pastor of his church, Hugh decided that his beliefs were Baptist and that the time was right for him to be baptised by total immersion.

The only place he wanted to be baptised was the only Baptist church where he had felt properly at home: that was Stony Stratford, the Baptist church he had found during his time in Wolverton, where E L Forster was still the minister. So Hugh continued his travels back to Stony Stratford where Forster welcomed him warmly.

Forster, in *The Freeman* many years later, remembered it in this way:

> Through his brother-in-law, one of our deacons, I learnt something about the state of his mind. I wrote to him and invited him to come and spend a month with me, when he could have the use of my study and library, and have time and quiet for the prosecution of his enquiries into this important subject. He gratefully and readily accepted my invitation, and came to be with us for a time.[15]

Hugh stayed with Forster and his family and during that time, in November 1846, Hugh was baptised, and that evening preached his first proper sermon, which he remembered as 'a poor one'. Forster remembers the order of events somewhat differently, suggesting that Hugh's baptism happened somewhat later, but he has clear memories of the occasion itself, and no criticism of Hugh's preaching that day:

> It was my privilege, for which I am grateful to my Saviour, the Head of the Church, to 'baptize him into the name of the Father, and the Son, and the Holy Ghost.' We had a three hours' service in our chapel

---

[15] *The Freeman*, 5th March 1886.

one Sunday evening. The place was crowded to excess. Numbers of his Wolverton friends hastened over to see and hear him tell how he had made up his mind to unite with the Baptists. He preached for an hour and a half, and then, after singing, prayer, and a short address, we went both of us down into the water, and I immersed him according to the Scriptural and primitive mode.[16]

Hugh discussed his future at length with his pastor and they decided that Hugh should enrol at Bristol Baptist College, the oldest and most respected Baptist college in the country. There Hugh would receive a good grounding in Baptist practice and evangelical Calvinist theology to add to his strong classical education.

There was another reason to be in Stony Stratford, and that was a young woman called Alice. Alice Chibnall Sirrett was the fifth daughter of John and Catherine Sirrett, though by the time Hugh knew her, her father had died. Alice was a year older than Hugh and as their relationship blossomed they must have planned ahead to Bristol college and beyond.

Tragedy at home

But, as was the pattern in Hugh's life, there was to be one more major twist before the couple could settle down together. A few days after his baptism, Hugh received a message that he was to hurry home. Hugh might have expected to hear that his father, Robert, was in worse

---

[16] Ibid.

health, but the news was of his brother, Robert junior. Robert had sailed out from Liverpool to Nassau in the Bahamas, and while he was there he had caught yellow fever and died, aged twenty-six. On top of this, another brother, Harry, aged fourteen, had caught gastric fever and was seriously ill. By the time Hugh reached the family home in Kirk Braddan, Harry had also died. It had been twenty years since the previous death in the family and now two sons had died suddenly. It was a hard blow to take for Robert, who was still not well himself. Hugh was now the eldest living child and the responsibility of care was suddenly his.

Hugh travelled to the Isle of Man to be with his grieving family, but he was eager to get back to Stony Stratford to be with Alice and his new family, and intended to stay there until going to the college in Bristol after Christmas. He stayed at home in Kirk Braddan for two weeks and in that time he cared for his father, took him for days out and told him stories. Robert went back to his work and Hugh bade his family farewell and took the carriage back to Douglas and then the steamer to Liverpool. It was a cold snowy late November Saturday and Hugh was glad to be travelling back in Liverpool, the first stage of another new start in life. He recalls that he attended Great George Street Chapel (now a community centre known as the Black-E) that Sunday morning and heard Liverpool's best-known nonconformist minister, Dr Thomas Raffles. From there he took a train to Forster's home in Stony Stratford, arriving on the Monday morning.

Forster tells the story, as he recalled it, in colourful terms:

Mr. Hugh ... remained with his parents some days, and then resolved to leave Douglas by the six o'clock packet on Saturday evening for Liverpool. His father's man-servant was to drive him to Douglas, a distance of about four miles. He had no sooner left than his father said to his mother, 'I think it is going to be a stormy night; I will go and stop Hugh from sailing.' This resolution was mysteriously and suddenly cut short by the Divine hand, and was never carried into effect. The servant saw Mr. Hugh on board, and the packet wend its way across the pathless waters. On his return there, sad sight! he saw his master lifeless on the road. He conveyed him to his home to the great grief of his beloved wife and family.

Mr. Hugh reached Liverpool in safety, and after a few hours' rest he started for Stony Stratford, which he reached about seven o'clock on Monday morning. I had not risen, and was, I suppose, a little Mondayish, having had three full services on the previous Sunday. My good wife was down stairs all alive, and busy as the honey bee. While I was snug in bed, and musing about the past day's work, I heard the well-known deep voice say, 'How do you do?' 'How do you do?' I sprang out of bed, and began dressing in a somewhat hurried fashion, when, lo, I heard a most lamentable and bitter cry. I rushed downstairs half-dressed to learn what was the matter. There was a letter which had just reached our house telling Hugh that his father had suddenly died on the road towards Douglas. Of course he hastened to the station to take the next train to

Liverpool, and thence to the Isle of Man, where his honoured father lay a corpse.[17]

Hugh himself, in his *Notes of My Life*, says that he received the letter from home with the news of his father's death on the Thursday after his return to Stony Stratford. Hugh left Stony Stratford immediately and was back at the vicarage by the evening of the next day. The following day Robert's funeral was held at Kirk Braddan Church and the family and the congregation mourned the death of the man who had himself buried many hundreds of members of their community over fourteen years at the church. The congregation at Kirk Braddan Church mourned their vicar Rev Robert Brown on Sunday 13th December 1846 when the traditional funeral sermon was preached by Rev Thomas Howard, rector of Ballaugh.

Robert Brown's grave can still be seen in the churchyard of Old Kirk Braddan. The inscription to Robert senior reads, 'UNDERNEATH repose the remains of THE REV ROBERT BROWN Vicar of this parish, who on the night of the 28th November 1846 was suddenly removed from the midst of his ministerial labours to his everlasting rest'. Poignantly, the death of his sons Henry (Harry) and Robert are marked on the same gravestone. Harry is buried with him, while the body of Robert junior was never returned from the Bahamas. Hugh's mother, Dorothy, and sister Dora rest alongside them in the adjoining plot.

---

[17] Ibid.

New responsibilities

Hugh was a man of his age, when the practical consequences of grief seemed to outweigh the raw emotions. One trait Hugh inherited from his father, Robert, was a constant concern about money, and after Robert's death money was a real concern. Dorothy was left alone with seven children. Hugh, now the eldest, would be considered old enough to earn his own income and bring some money into the family, except that after three attempts at entering a trade, he was jobless and penniless. The next in age, Will, was already an apprentice in the merchant navy, but he was not earning anything like enough to send money home to his mother. There were five others at home: Dora, aged seventeen, unmarried and a help around the house; Tom, the studious one, at King William's College; Margaret, aged twelve; Harriet, aged ten; and little Alfred, just turning seven.

Thankfully Robert had been careful with money and had left no debts, unlike most country parsons of his time. But the home Dorothy and the children lived in belonged to the Church, and would be needed for the next curate at Kirk Braddan. There was no pension and no source of income. The only place to live was for them all to squeeze in with Dorothy's unmarried sister in Castletown. The parishioners were generous and raised some finances, so the family could afford to move, and after that it was a future that relied on charity and any contributions Hugh could provide.

For Hugh it was one more setback to his plans. Enrolling at Bristol college was no longer possible, and the prospect of being near the support of Forster and Stony Stratford

Chapel, and indeed Alice, seemed unlikely. One thing that was never shaken was Hugh's firm faith in the God who was leading him and supporting him. Hugh reasoned that if his Lord was using these recent tragic circumstances to bring him back to his family, then this was the place he should be seeking to serve God in Christian ministry. If his ordination had gone ahead just a few months earlier then perhaps he could have taken over his father's position as curate at Kirk Braddan. Then his mother and his sisters and brothers could have stayed in the same house. But this door had been firmly closed.

The nearest thing to a Baptist church in the Isle of Man was the Independent chapel in Douglas, and Hugh joined their cause. The minister, a Mr Harrison, asked Hugh to share his work and Hugh started conducting worship and preaching on a few Sunday evenings. The people of the church received his preaching well. Then another opportunity seemed to open up. A Methodist chapel building in the north of Douglas was not being used, and by March 1847 Hugh was starting to negotiate the use of the building to hold Baptist services. But the new church plant was never to come to birth. Instead a letter from Liverpool was to offer a new enticing opportunity, and yet another new start.

4
Coming to Liverpool

The letter Hugh Stowell Brown received was from Myrtle Street Baptist chapel in Liverpool, a Baptist church from a long tradition of Baptist worship in the town.

Myrtle Street Baptist Church was as old as the century. Its origins went back to the earliest Baptist church in Liverpool in the seventeenth century. The Baptist movement dates back to 1609 when a group of English Christians calling themselves Separatists were baptised as believers in Amsterdam. They'd gone to Holland seeking religious freedom, because in England they were not allowed to have any Christian meeting that was not in the Church of England. Their leader, John Smyth, took the bold step of baptising himself and then baptised the other church members. They returned to England in 1612 under the leadership of Thomas Helwys and settled at Spitalfields near the Tower of London.

By 1625 there were Baptists in Tiverton, Norwich, Coventry and Salisbury. The Baptist Movement spread with the growth and movement of the Parliamentarian army during the civil war. Wherever Cromwell's army went, Baptist churches were founded. By 1649 there was a Baptist congregation in Frodsham and at the same time Hill Cliffe Baptist Church near Warrington was founded, and this became the mother church of many others in Cheshire and Lancashire.

Baptists in Liverpool

After the restoration of the monarchy in 1660 and until the Toleration Act of 1689 Baptists were persecuted and driven out of centres of population. When a physician called Dr Fabius and his wife (or in some accounts his sister), Hannah, moved to Liverpool from Holland in 1689, he came to be the pastor of a small group of Baptists in Everton. It is said that Fabius' real name was Mr Bean, but he Latinised it as Dr Fabius to give some extra dignity to his role as the only medical practitioner in Everton. He lived in a house at the top of Brunswick Road and was involved in the building of the first Baptist chapel in Liverpool and the first place of worship in the Everton 'township' in 1705, when it had a membership of thirty-five. The congregation increased and found a better meeting place in Byrom Street in the town of Liverpool in 1722 and the Everton chapel was abandoned.

Baptist churches, although congregational and independent by government, have always met together for fellowship and strategic planning. In 1722 an Association of Baptist churches from across the counties of Lancashire and Yorkshire met in Liverpool, the fourth such meeting of 'messengers' or delegates from Baptist churches. The teaching of these churches was Calvinist, emphasising the sovereignty of God and His grace in choosing people rather than any merit of faith within a believer. This was in keeping with the spirit of the age, which was rationalist, emphasising the search for truth through reason rather than faith or experience.

In 1741 a man in his mid-thirties called John Johnson was called to pastor the Liverpool Baptist Church. Johnson's views were 'hyper-Calvinist' and he created division wherever he went. Many churches in Lancashire and Cheshire split under his influence and joined the High Calvinist Northern Association. This signalled the cessation of the Yorkshire and Lancashire Baptist Association for a generation. Johnson left the church in 1748 and formed his own congregation. A remnant of this group was still meeting in Comus Street in 1886, but the hyper-Calvinist movement set back the progress of Baptists across the whole of northern England.

Medley the hymn-writer

The next and most significant turning point in the Baptist cause in Liverpool came in 1772 when Samuel Medley came to be the pastor of the struggling church meeting in the chapel in Byrom Street. Samuel Medley's father had been a friend of Sir Isaac Newton. Medley set out on a career in the navy, rising to the rank of master's mate, but had to leave the navy because of a severe leg injury incurred in a sea battle against the French. He came under the influence of George Whitefield and felt a call to preach, first in Watford and then among the seafaring community of Liverpool. Much of his work in Liverpool was among sailors, both on the docks and in the church, where he built up a large congregation, predominantly of sailors and young people. Medley worked in Liverpool, from 1772 until his death in 1799. During his time Byrom Street chapel was enlarged in 1773 and rebuilt in 1789.

Later generations referred to Medley as 'the hymn-writer'. He wrote at least 230 hymns of which many have been included in collections, particularly among more Calvinistic churches. One of Medley's best-known hymns is 'I Know That My Redeemer Lives', written in 1775:

> I know that my Redeemer lives;
> What comfort this sweet sentence gives!
> He lives, He lives, who once was dead;
> He lives, my ever living Head.
>
> He lives to bless me with His love,
> He lives to plead for me above.
> He lives my hungry soul to feed,
> He lives to help in time of need.
>
> He lives triumphant from the grave,
> He lives eternally to save,
> He lives all glorious in the sky,
> He lives exalted there on high.[18]

The dawning of the nineteenth century, one that was to be dominated by Hugh Stowell Brown, brought with it dissension and vision among Liverpool's Baptists. Another movement towards High Calvinism, which damaged the unity of the church, had marked the last years of Medley's life. On Medley's death in 1799 the Byrom Street church was left not only bereaved and bereft but also divided over doctrinal matters. Rev Richard Davies was called to be the

---

[18] Samuel Medley (1738-99), public domain.

pastor at Byrom Street but twenty-two of the members of the church disagreed with his appointment and left to form their own church, meeting in Church Lane. This group, now numbering forty-four, appointed Rev Peter Aitken to be their pastor in April 1801, but eleven of their number disagreed with this appointment and began a new church, meeting in Mathew Street. Then in October 1801 Peter Aitken died. In June 1803 the Church Lane group appointed James Lister of Glasgow to be their pastor. At the same time they built a new chapel in Lime Street at the cost of £1,900. In October 1803 the Lime Street Church and its new minister began the ministry which was to precede that of Hugh Stowell Brown.

Byrom Street chapel continued through the first half of the nineteenth century, though by the time of Brown the building no longer held regular worship but was used as a 'mission station' in what was by then a densely populated part of the town. In 1838 the wealthier members of Byrom Street had left with their minister Charles Birrell to form another new church, Pembroke Chapel, in Pembroke Place, which although notionally Baptist was independently minded and offered communion and membership to those who had not been baptised. Pembroke Chapel was described to Hugh Stowell Brown by his brother as a 'horrid schism shop',[19] but it was also the centre of a notable preaching ministry and from 1869 one of its ministers was the world-famous preacher F B Meyer.

---

[19] Hugh Stowell Brown, ed W S Caine, *Notes of My Life*, in *Hugh Stowell Brown, A Memorial Volume*, p 70.

The excellent Mr Lister

Under the ministry of James Lister the new church in Lime Street prospered. Lister was a 'Fullerite', a Particular Baptist in the tradition of Andrew Fuller of Kettering, who had led a movement in the late eighteenth century away from the hyper-Calvinism of Johnson and others. His pamphlet *The Gospel Worthy of All Acceptation* set forth an evangelical Christianity which was to set the tone for Free Church life in the nineteenth century and beyond. Fuller's teaching was practical and evangelistic. He spoke of the role of the Holy Spirit in conversion and, although he believed that God chose people for salvation, he stressed the need to challenge people to turn to Christ in faith. This middle way between Arminianism and the blind alley of hyper-Calvinism allowed James Lister, and Hugh Stowell Brown after him, to find a theological position that gave a new confidence to Baptists in the new world of the nineteenth century.

Writing about the history of Myrtle Street chapel in 1873, Brown spoke warmly of James Lister as the man on whose giant's shoulders he stood. Brown wrote of Lister:

> He was a man of learning and piety; a careful student and an excellent expositor of scripture, whom with all his mind believed and all his heart loved and with all his might preached the great truth of evangelical religion.[20]

---

[20] Hugh Stowell Brown, *A Quarter of a Century in the Non Conformist Ministry* (London: Yates and Alexander, 1873), p 3.

By 1809 Lime Street Church had grown to ninety members and by 1818 to over 150. The church started a Sunday school in March 1816 in a room in Bolton Street, with an initial compliment of eighteen teachers and fifty-four 'scholars'. The chapel was extended to make room for the Sunday school in about 1820.

Through the 1830s Lime Street was at the centre of the development of Liverpool. The corporation had started buying up land to build a new railway station in 1833. In 1836 the new railway station, still in use today, was opened. By 1841 traffic around the new station had become so heavy that more improvements were needed, and one of the casualties of the development was Lime Street chapel. The town corporation bought up the chapel which allowed the membership to build a bigger chapel in the newly developing area of Myrtle Street, on the corner of Hope Street. This was time of grand building projects in Liverpool and the neighbouring Philharmonic Hall on Hope Street was opened in 1849.

Myrtle Street chapel rises

On 4th October 1842, the foundation stone of Myrtle Street chapel was laid, and on Wednesday 10th January 1844 the building was opened for worship. James Lister had been minister of the church from its difficult beginnings more than forty years before, and the move to the grand new chapel in Myrtle Street was the crowning glory of his long and fruitful ministry.

Commemorative china marking the opening of Myrtle Street chapel (photo: Rev Dr David Steers, velvethummingbee.wordpress.com, used by permission)

Hugh Stowell Brown was to reflect twenty-five years later: 'Mr Lister sowed and I reaped.'[21] In March 1847 James Lister, failing in health, laid down his ministry. He had served the church for forty-four years. Those years had been marked by growth, but most remarkably they had been marked by retaining unity within a church which had such a history of dissension and division.

Later that same month, Saturday 27th March 1847, Hugh, aged twenty-three, crossed the Irish Sea to Liverpool, and a new chapter of his life was beginning. At the time he was more concerned with the rough crossing on a stormy night. In response to an invitation from the church secretary, a local surgeon called G Godfrey, he had

---

[21] Ibid, p 4.

endured the difficult journey to preach morning and evening at Myrtle Street chapel. Liverpool was a busy port and the main point of contact between the Isle of Man and England, so Brown had been through Liverpool a number of times before but he had never got to know the town. He records that he 'did not know any person in this town', nor was he aware of any Baptist chapel. He says he 'did not know of the existence of Myrtle Street chapel, or of Myrtle Street itself'.

Although the invitation was to preach morning and evening, on his arrival Brown discovered that Mr Godfrey had bigger ideas. Myrtle Street was without a pastor and Godfrey was already thinking that this untried Manx preacher might be the right person to lead the church.

If he had shared this vision with the untried preacher, he would probably have turned around and gone home. As it was, just seeing the chapel nearly scared him away. He comments, 'the idea of my preaching in such a place was almost too much for me'. He was stunned by the scale and the beauty of the interior of the chapel, still only three years old. Adornments he didn't like were the chandeliers, enormous structures weighing two tons each.

The first Sunday

Myrtle Street was barely half full that cold and damp morning, but that still amounted to nearly 500 people. Brown's nervousness at facing the rows of strangers sitting in the pews on Sunday 28th March was only alleviated by the thought that, as he was a young visiting preacher only there to 'supply the pulpit', no one would be bold enough to criticise him. If he spoke badly then he could return to the Island and chalk up his fleeting visit to Liverpool as experience. As he stood looking down at the expectant faces he could hardly have imagined how this day was going to change his life. He was twenty-three years old and had preached no more than a dozen sermons in his life. He had been a convinced Baptist for six months and the only Baptist minister he knew was the man who had baptised him.

It would be fitting to report that Brown's first sermon at Myrtle Street was magnificent and drew admiration from his listeners, but it wasn't. He spoke from memory, having spent many hours preparing the fine themes and finer words he would deliver. His text was 'It is Finished', the dying words spoken by Jesus from the cross recorded in John 19:30. Drawing on many years of hearing his father speak on the cross of Christ, he attempted to describe the effects of the death of Christ.

With a little more experience Brown soon realised that the best way to reach people's hearts in preaching was to use simple, down-to-earth language, but this eager young man thought he could impress his educated congregation with flowery words and long swooping sentences. Speaking to the stars he said:

> Are there no mysteries among you, ye stars of night? Have ye no inhabitants who are the object of a creator's love? Wherefore, then, do ye hang upon His arm and roll around His feet?[22]

---

[22] Hugh Stowell Brown, ed W S Caine, *Notes of My Life*, in *Hugh Stowell Brown, A Memorial Volume*, p 74.

He asked the world in general:

Wherefore was this den of traitors suffered to continue in existence? Wherefore was this world not driven from the universe?[23]

He called out to his by now bemused listeners:

Oh how would Satan have exulted had he beheld the forceps of God's wrath grasping the world by its poles and hurling it into hell![24]

The sermon was building to a soaring climax as the young man declared:

It is finished; blessed proclamation: earth listened to the sound, and trembled while it listened! Heaven heard the all-potent words, and gathered up its clouds and looked cheerfully on the earth again, and the clouds rolled themselves away like the smoke of battle when the fight is ended! It struck on Satan's ear and he turned pale to hear a voice laden with the destruction of his power. It ran through the armies of the angels and a shout of victory rang through the courts of heaven and it was answered with deep groans from hell![25]

Writing more than thirty years later, Brown described with disdain his first attempt at impressing the fine congregation of Myrtle Street. He was critical of his poor efforts to be 'eloquent, grand, impressive, powerful', and

---

[23] Ibid, p 74.
[24] Ibid, p 75.
[25] Ibid, p 75.

indeed the sermon verges on the ridiculous in its efforts to imitate the great rhetoric of an earlier age. But, to its credit, Brown's approach to his text is bold and mature. He isn't satisfied with a theology of the cross which is just about personal salvation and fulfilment, such the one seen in Isaac Watts' hymn of 1707:

> When I survey the wondrous cross
> Where the young the Prince of Glory died
> My richest gain I count but loss
> And pour contempt on all my pride.[26]

For Brown the death of Christ was of cosmic significance, an event that shook earth, heaven and hell. Even at an early age the scope of his preaching was mature, seeing faith not as matter of private fulfilment but public truth. It's also worth noting Brown's reference to the 'stars of night' that might have 'inhabitants who are the objects of a creator's love'. This was an idea ahead of its time in 1847. The leaders of the church received Brown's clumsy efforts at rhetoric with a generous spirit. One man later admitted he was laughing behind his hand at the phrase 'the forceps of God's wrath grasping the world by its poles', but many still returned in the evening to hear him again. The evening sermon was more measured and delivered in language that was more in keeping with his later reputation for plain speaking. Brown described it as 'not so skiey nor so starry as the other'. The young preacher must have impressed his listeners with his evening sermon more than the first one, or perhaps people saw something

---

[26] Isaac Watts (1674-1748), public domain.

in the young Hugh which went beyond the words he delivered. He was immediately asked to return the following Sunday and preach morning and evening again, as the man booked to come from Manchester had been taken ill. He spent the intervening week getting to know the church and its members and started to imagine what it would be like to be invited to their pastor. His preaching the second Sunday was an improvement on the previous week and the church began to appreciate the young man's pastoral heart as well as his obvious gifts as a preacher.

Invited to return

Brown returned to the Isle of Man, and in July a letter arrived from Mr Godfrey on behalf of the church, inviting the inexperienced, untrained Manx preacher to take up a probationary period of three months as pastor of Myrtle Street Baptist Church. In accordance with Baptist practice a meeting of the church members had discussed the invitation and had agreed to the trial period without any opposition, though it was reported that the resolution was carried 'quietly and seriously'.

In August 1847 Hugh Stowell Brown embarked upon what must have been a nervous three months, still not quite believing what was happening to him. In November the church had to meet to vote again on a resolution that they invite Brown to be their permanent pastor. At this stage there was a significant minority who voted against the resolution, including two of the deacons. But the large majority wanted Brown to continue the good work he had started. A few of the minority who dissented from the church's call to ministry subsequently left the church, but most stayed at the church and became loyal friends.

Hugh Stowell Brown, 1848, aged twenty-four (photo: public domain)

Brown accepted the church's call and declared, 'one of the greatest questions of my life was settled'. He was still only twenty-four, with little experience of preaching and none of pastoral work and, as he admitted, 'a very slender amount of knowledge'. Only twelve months after deciding his convictions led him to being a Baptist, he was now pastor of one of the largest Baptist churches in a location as significant as Liverpool.

5
Church Life

Hugh Stowell Brown was minister of Myrtle Street Baptist Church from 1847 to his death in 1886, just short of forty years. In that time it grew in numbers and influence, largely because of the fame and influence of its minister. A print from an engraving of the church appeared in the *Illustrated News of the World* in August 1858, not with the title 'Myrtle Street Chapel' but 'THE REV. HUGH STOWELL BROWN'S CHAPEL, LIVERPOOL'. Brown had been minister at Myrtle Street for only ten years, but at that time a London newspaper reproduced a picture of the church because of the reputation of its minister.

1847 was the peak year of Irish immigration to Liverpool at the height of the potato famine. In the first half of that year about 300,000 people came into Liverpool from Ireland and about half of those stayed in the town. It could be claimed that the character of Liverpool changed more in 1847 than in any other year in its 800-year history. By the end of 1847 there were 35,000 people, mainly Irish, living in cellars in the worst conditions ever seen in the town. Most of these were in Vauxhall and Scotland Road, less than two miles from the chapel and its manse in Myrtle Street.

1847 was also the year that Dr William Duncan was appointed Liverpool's Medical Officer of Health, the first such appointment in Britain. Dr Duncan recognised that there was a link between the poor housing conditions in the town and the outbreak of diseases such as cholera, smallpox and typhus.

Brown's first service at Myrtle Street was on 2nd January 1848, and it was a baptism service. Three people were baptised, and the first was a Mrs Caine. This may have been the wife of Nathaniel Caine, the mother of William and Phoebe Caine and so the lady who was later to become Hugh's mother-in-law. But there were other Caines in the church including the parents of Sir Hall Caine, one of the best-loved novelists of the late nineteenth century.

Welcomed and ordained

On Wednesday 1st March Hugh Stowell Brown was 'ordained to the pastoral office' in Myrtle Street chapel. It was, and still is, normal for Baptist ministers to be ordained once their ministry has been recognised by the call of a local church. Although it was a weekday there were two services that day and the chapel was crowded with people for the significant occasion. The church minute-book records that congregations were large for both services and 'the Great Head of the Church was experienced in our midst'.

At 11 am the service was led by Rev Lancaster of Soho Street Baptist Chapel, and Rev Henry Dowson, the historian and minister of Westgate Chapel, Bradford, and secretary of Horton Academy, stated the 'nature, order, obligations and privileges of a gospel church' from

Ephesians 4:4-6. Dowson then asked 'the usual questions of Mr Brown – his conversion, experience, doctrinal views and views of the ministry', and then asked a member of the church to state the 'leadings of providence' in the call of their new minister.

The ordination prayer, it is recorded, was 'stern and impressive', and hands were laid on Brown by Dowson, Lancaster and by a man the minutes call 'Rev W Swan of Birmingham', who may have been the great anti-slavery campaigner Thomas Swan, at that time minister of Cannon Street chapel in Birmingham. Swan was the main preacher that morning, speaking on the challenges of the work of the pastoral office from 2 Corinthians 2 with the text 'Who is sufficient for these things?'

The celebrations continued in the evening when a service was led by Dr Raffles from Great George Street Chapel, the first preacher Brown had ever heard in Liverpool, and the sermon was delivered by the man who became Brown's closest friend, Charles Birrell of Pembroke Chapel. The service was closed by Rev Dr Verner M White, minister at the Presbyterian Church at Islington, Liverpool.

Although Brown had been preaching at Myrtle Street since March 1847 and had become their permanent minister in January 1848 it is apparent that it was not thought right for him to conduct communion services until he was ordained. In February 1848 James Lister is still 'presiding at the Lord's table' and Brown's first communion service is on the first Sunday after his ordination, 5th March 1848, six months after he started his probationary term, and more than two months after he has been working as the permanent pastor of the church.

When Brown was added to the membership roll at Myrtle Street in 1847 the church had 239 members. In the first four years of Brown's time as minister the church added to its membership – twenty-eight in the first year, then thirty-one, thirty-seven and forty-two new members in the next three years. This is remarkable given that Brown arrived just after the retirement of the much-loved former minister James Lister, and it might have been expected that some of the members of Myrtle Street wouldn't take to the new, young, inexperienced replacement for their beloved elder statesman of a pastor. In fact, Hugh always spoke well of James Lister, from whom he learned a lot in the four years the old man lived after his retirement. Hugh admired Lister for his discipline of study and scholarship, and his caring pastoral heart, although he was feared by some for his stern appearance.

Just before Lister died in 1851 he wrote a letter to the church and shared his 'delight in the prosperity which attended the Church, in the increase of members and the increase of hearers, and in the union and harmony which has been maintained'.[27]

The expanding church

By May 1851 Hugh was married and his family was rapidly expanding with a third child already expected. Myrtle Street chapel also needed to be expanded to make room for the increased congregation. This involved adding side galleries to the main sanctuary at considerable cost

---

[27] Quoted in Hugh Stowell Brown, ed W S Caine, *Notes of My Life*, in *Hugh Stowell Brown, A Memorial Volume*, p 130.

THE REV. HUGH STOWELL BROWN'S CHAPEL, LIVERPOOL.

Myrtle Street chapel, as featured in *Illustrated News of the World*, 14th August 1858 (photo: public domain)

and inconvenience. The building was just seven years old when the work was carried out and Hugh was never happy with the result. He recorded in his memoirs, 'we accumulated our funds and spoiled our chapel by the erection of the side-galleries at the cost of £400'. He does add, however, that some good came of the building work as the 'hideous chandeliers' were removed and replaced with powerful gas lamps called 'sun-burners'.

In 1859, only eight years after side galleries were added to the building, more expansion work was necessary. On 25th September of that year the church celebrated its reopening after alterations and enlargements that meant the loss of the chapel's lecture hall, though it retained a smaller hall where prayer meetings were held. Those alterations cost the princely sum of £4,400. Between 1851 and 1859 another 260 members had been added to the church, an average of about thirty-two each year.

Brown recorded in 1868 that of the 239 people who had been in membership when he joined the church twenty years earlier, only seventy-five people remained in membership. Most of the others had died, though some had moved to other churches.

The church finances continued to thrive through Brown's ministry and this was reflected in the amount the minister was paid. On his appointment the church agreed to pay him an annual salary (salary is the word that is used, not stipend) of £250. In 1851 this was raised to £300 and in 1855 to £500 a year. In 1865 this was raised again to £900, and by this time it is believed that Brown was being paid more than any other Dissenting minister in Britain. When Brown's friend Alexander Maclaren became president of the Baptist Union in 1875 he argued for a fund to bring the minimum ministerial stipend for a Baptist minister to £120 a year. In the 1860s an engineer in the profession Brown had left behind might be paid £110 a year for a ten-hour day and six-day working week, and a civil service officer £300 a year. Brown would have paid from his salary the cost of preachers who filled the pulpit while he was away, and he did regularly open his home to others in hospitality, but he was undeniably very well paid.

Writing in 1868, Brown reflected that although the building expansion of 1859 had created more space, it had deprived the building of a facility he valued. He wrote: 'They robbed us of our old Lecture Hall, or at all events left it the dark and useless place that it is now. We must lecture now where we hold our prayer meetings.'[28] It seems that the extension had taken the natural light from the hall where the weekday services were held and where Brown would deliver his series of evening teaching sessions for the church.

Brown also regretted that, although the church now had three times the numbers of members it had when he began and four times the size of congregation, the numbers attending the prayer meetings were fewer than they had been then. This, he considered, was because of the distance that people lived from the chapel. Many of the people in the church were no longer living in the town centre. Some were travelling to Myrtle Street on a Sunday from a distance away, presumably because of the appeal of the famous preacher. Others had moved out of the town centre as they had increased in wealth and as the suburbs of Liverpool had grown. Many, he reflected, who once lived within ten minutes' walk of the chapel, now lived well out of town.

Another reason for fewer people attending midweek church activities, Brown reasoned, was the increased number of alternative options for people to use their time.

---

[28] Ibid, p 82.

The options he had in mind were not worldly alternatives to the prayer meeting but 'public meetings in aid of religious objects' – Christian philanthropy, Ragged Schools, evening classes, cottage meetings and home visitation.

A growing network

The increased movement of people out of the town centre, and the continuing attraction of Myrtle Street, led the church to develop a network of meeting places and missions beyond its own walls. Alongside an expansion of its own membership, Myrtle Street under the leadership of Hugh Stowell Brown developed a policy of what is currently known as 'church planting'. Although that term wasn't used in the nineteenth century, the missionary methods that are popular in our generation were being encouraged by Brown.

His opinion was that numbers of believers shouldn't travel to Myrtle Street for their Sunday worship but that, having come to faith in Christ, they should form satellite churches where they lived. People routinely travelled many miles to hear Brown preach, but Hugh discouraged any reliance on him and wanted people to be witnesses to their own communities. Through his insistence, many churches were set up by Myrtle Street in other places during his ministry, and this practice continued to be the policy of Myrtle Street for at least twenty years after his death.

The first 'mission station' from Myrtle Street was set up in Mill Street in Liverpool in 1849, when Brown had been pastor at Myrtle Street for less than two years. Mill Street is in Toxteth Park, not far from the much larger Toxteth Tabernacle Baptist Church which was built on Park Road in 1871.

Churches such as Mill Street began meeting in a home but soon the money was raised to build their own chapel. At first those attending the mission station would be on the membership roll at Myrtle Street. Their worship would not include communion and they would not have their own minister, but services would be led by lay preachers from Myrtle Street and a deacon at Myrtle Street would be the leader of the mission station. The next phase in the life of the new church plant would usually be for it to have its own minister and to begin to hold its own communion services, and then its own baptism services. The final stage would be for it to be established as a church in its own right with a separate membership, who would be commissioned and released from Myrtle Street to form the new membership of the newly constituted church.

A further complication is that some churches already existed when Myrtle Street took them under its wing, so they became mission stations of Myrtle Street but already had their own buildings, memberships and histories. Dating the foundation of a 'new church' is not always easy, because the date may refer to the date a congregation started meeting or the date the building was opened, or the date the church became independent, or some date in between.

Other mission stations opened in different parts of Liverpool, notably churches in Solway Street and Juno Street, then one at Princes Gate.

Solway Street Church, south of Upper Parliament Street, began in 1867 and the small chapel was enlarged three times: in 1868, 1874 and 1884. Juno Street no longer exists, but was near Edge Hill railway station. A chapel was opened there as a branch of Myrtle Street in May 1878. Then a Baptist chapel was opened in the Toxteth Park area by Princes Park gates called Princes Gate Baptist Church. The minute-books record that twenty-six members of Myrtle Street were released in March 1881 to membership of Princes Gate when the chapel was opened, led by a Mr and Mrs Godfrey, possibly the same Mr Godfrey, a surgeon, who had invited Brown to preach at Myrtle Street back in 1847.

Princes Gate Church is described by Nikolaus Pevsner in his *South Lancashire, the Industrial and Commercial South* as being designed by Henry Summers and built 1879 to 1881. Pevsner, in the 1969 edition, considered the building to be remarkable with some distinctive features.[29] The church had some outstanding leaders through nearly 100 years of service and was closed and demolished in 1974.

None of these Liverpool churches planted in Brown's time have lasted until the present day. Other churches such as Toxteth Tabernacle have continued, and Dovedale Baptist Church, planted by Myrtle Street in the following generation, closed in 2018. Most of the places where Brown planted churches in Liverpool were in his time the areas of population growth, but since then the population has moved further out of the city centre to parts that did not exist in his time.

---

[29] Nikolaus Pevsner, *The Buildings of England: Lancashire 1, the Industrial and Commercial South*, first edition (London: Penguin, 1969), p 245.

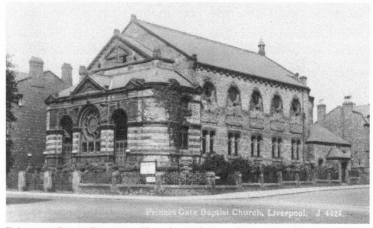

Princes Gate Baptist Church (photo: Rev Dr David Steers, velvethummingbee.wordpress.com, used by permission)

The church outside Liverpool

Beyond Liverpool there was much interest in the work of Myrtle Street and its famous preacher-pastor. While churches in Liverpool were mainly planted as mission enterprises – opportunities for growth and evangelism in new population centres – most of the churches beyond Liverpool that became part of Myrtle Street came about through small existing groups looking to Brown for his help and support, not least his financial help.

The Baptist church at St Helens began when a group of Christians from Laffak, a village on the East Lancs Road north of St Helens, fifteen miles from Liverpool, came to Myrtle Street in May 1862 and asked Brown for baptism and membership of the church. Twenty-two of them were baptised the following month but were encouraged to meet in their own town. The money for the building project was provided by a Mr Shanks and in 1866 a chapel was built in Park Road, St Helens, and opened on 25th September 1869.

The St Helens church remained a branch church of Myrtle Street for many years after and the mother church employed a pastor, Rev W C Tayler, who served the St Helens church alongside the church at Earlestown. By 1884 St Helens had a membership of 106 and was the largest of any of the mission stations or affiliated churches.

From 1888 to 1890 its pastor was Charles F Aked, who soon moved on to Pembroke Chapel, Liverpool. After receiving a Doctor of Divinity degree from Temple College, Pennsylvania, Aked accepted the invitation to be pastor of 'the Millionaires' Church' of Fifth Avenue Baptist Church in New York in 1906, known as the Rockefeller Church, heavily endowed by John D Rockefeller, the richest man in the world. By 1912 Charles had moved on to the First Congregational Church in San Francisco. He later went to Kansas City and finally to All Souls' Church, Los Angeles. He was described by one journal as 'the greatest living pulpit orator'.

Ralph Hall Caine, brother of the novelist Thomas Hall Caine, remembers the influence of Brown and the preaching of Aked at St Helens in his book *Isle of Man*:

> [Brown] was the Spurgeon of the North of England, where, towards the end of an entirely useful and honourable career, one of his lieutenants at a little branch church near St. Helens, in Lancashire, was the brilliant-minded, silver-tongued Rev. Charles F. Aked, now of Fifth Avenue Baptist Church, New

York, and his organist, a master of melody, was Mr.
W. H. Jude, whose songs are so widely known.[30]

W H (William Herbert) Jude (1851–1922) was widely known as one of the greatest organists of his time. He was organist for the Blue Coat School and concert hall in Liverpool and in great demand for recitals. He is the writer of hymn-tunes such as 'Galilee', used for the hymn 'Jesus Calls Us o'er the Tumult'.

The current Baptist church in St Helens is still thriving and, having amalgamated with other churches, sees its roots in the small group who were baptised in 1862.

There was a similar story at Warrington, seventeen miles from Liverpool, when a group of Baptists meeting at Rylands Street in the town came to Myrtle Street in 1871 wanting to be a branch church. This group gained the support of Myrtle Street to build a chapel in Golborne Street, opened on 2nd August 1876, and on 26th February 1879 the members applied to Myrtle Street to become a separate church in their own right. The church met in the Golborne Street chapel until the 1970s when they moved to a new building.

In the town of Widnes, some thirteen miles from Liverpool, the Baptist church similarly owes its beginnings to Myrtle Street. In January 1872 twelve people from Widnes came to Brown seeking baptism. Individuals from Myrtle Street and from Widnes contributed to cost of building a Baptist chapel there. Their first pastor was Rev Joseph Fairbank but he resigned in 1877, and in 1884 its

[30] W Ralph Hall Caine, *Isle of Man* (London: Adam and Charles Black, 1909), p 211.

thirty-four members welcomed their second pastor, Rev R Yeatman. The neo-Gothic, red-brick chapel, opened on 25th July 1873, is still in use today and the church is still small but active.

In 1875 a group from Earlestown, fifteen miles from Liverpool, approached Brown. Since October 1871 a group calling themselves the 'Baptist Friends' had been meeting. Five local men, George Cuffin, Joseph Eckersley, Joseph Gibbons, John Wallington and John Walton, had felt led to act upon their faith and hired an upstairs room in Market Street, in the town centre for worship 'according to the principles and practices of the Baptists'. They needed funding and spiritual support and Myrtle Street offered them both, and the group became a branch church of Myrtle Street. In 1880 they accepted W C Tayler as their pastor, shared with Park Road, St Helens, and in 1881 they opened what Brown calls 'an exceedingly neat chapel'. By 1884 their membership stood at seventy-six. The old chapel closed in the year 2000 but was replaced with the Crownway Community Centre, a facility for all the community owned and run by the church.

Myrtle Street was also involved in opening and supporting Baptist churches in New Ferry in Wirral, in Aughton, ten miles north of Liverpool, and in Prescot, eight miles to the east. These last two began late in Brown's ministry in 1879 and 1884 respectively.

Growing in numbers

The minute-books that record the proceedings of church meetings and deacons' meetings from the time Hugh

Stowell Brown was minister at Myrtle Street reveal details of the life of the church, and are also revealing in what they do not record. There are no mentions, for instance, of the pastor's tour to America other than a reference to a committee that was raising money for the trip, and nothing at all about Brown's year as president of the Baptist Union.

What they do record are the number of baptisms being held in the church. The number and names of people being baptised run through the church minutes with great consistency. People were being baptised on Sunday mornings, Sunday evenings and some Wednesdays, at least once a month and sometimes week after week during Brown's years at the church, except for the weeks he was away. It seems that Brown liked to conduct all the baptisms himself.

The minutes are full of numbers: numbers of people baptised, numbers of members, dates and figures. We learn that the 'chapel keeper' for twenty-seven years, William Gee was paid an annual salary of only £80 when the pastor was being paid £900, but that after Mr Gee's death the church paid the £13 cost of his funeral and grave, and continued to employ Mrs Gee in the work.

The year of greatest growth in numbers was 1875. In this year the church added 128 members including eighty-six by baptism and twenty-seven by 'profession' – those who became Christians but were not baptised. This was a year of great spiritual fervour in Liverpool, the year that Moody and Sankey came to the town with their revival crusade. The American evangelists Dwight Moody and Ira Sankey had arrived in Liverpool in 1873 but it wasn't until February 1875 that they began public meetings in the town at the end of their British tour. Their meetings attracted crowds of up to 2,000 people. Brown wasn't directly involved in the crusade meetings and didn't enjoy their style, considering them too emotional. But he did acknowledge the way people had come to faith in Christ through the meetings. He attributed ten of the new converts at Myrtle Street to the preaching of D L Moody, but the record number of people baptised that year would suggest that more were influenced by his preaching or by the mood of revival that was around in the town that year.

The hard-working pastor

Over the years Brown continued in his weekly pattern of work: rising early to read the Bible and putting many hours of preparation into his talks, typically a Sunday morning sermon, a Sunday evening sermon, a short reflection to begin the Monday evening prayer meeting, and the Wednesday evening Bible exposition that he called a lecture. Often he was also speaking on a Sunday afternoon and a Saturday as well, and maybe addressing a public meeting for some good cause on another evening. He took all of these public speaking engagements very seriously and prepared for them thoroughly, so he could speak as much as possible without notes.

In his *Commonplace Book* in early 1876 he writes:

I call to-day's work pretty full. Morning service as usual. Afternoon a baptismal service, with address. Perhaps 700 present; several young people baptized. Evening the usual service, and after that to Solwey [sic] Street on foot, and Lord's Supper administration there all by myself. Came home not in the least tired, and ate a mighty supper and sat talking and reading, and walking about the dining room until after 1a.m. It was certainly twelve hours of incessant work – brain, heart and voice. And I never felt better than I do now after it.

In these services the prayers of course are extempore, and the preaching without a scrap of paper or note of any kind, so that the mind is on the stretch all through the day. I think some of our prayer and sermon reading parsons would be in a fix if they had to do quarter as much as I do every Sunday of life. I have been able to do this without a break for twenty-eight years – *Laus Deo!*[31]

We are given the names and addresses of the seven deacons – lay leaders – who were in post in 1877 including Thomas Gibson of 51 Oxford Street, the 'senior deacon', Nathaniel Caine and Thomas Mounsey. They are, of course, all men, and all have addresses in the substantial streets of the town centre, suggesting they were upper-middle class wealthy people of some social status. In this year it was decided more deacons were needed and one of the newly elected men was William Caine, by then thirty-five years old and still working for his father Nathaniel's company, though Nathaniel died later that same year.

With a large church and only a few deacons, the workload on Brown was heavy. As well as speaking commitments, there were deacons' meetings, other business meetings and endless committees to attend.

---

[31] Hugh Stowell Brown, ed W S Caine, *Extracts from His Commonplace Book*, in *Hugh Stowell Brown, A Memorial Volume*, p 168.

Brown was also very attentive to pastoral visiting; this was mainly done on foot and increasingly the congregation were living at a greater distance from the church and from his home. He also had many letters to write, and he reports that the number of correspondents rose as he became better known. He accepted many invitations to speak, but declined more than he accepted and each one had to be replied to. His *Commonplace Book* also records many 'callers' – people who turned up at the church or at his home wanting his attention, all of whom needed to be given some time.

Illness strikes

What seems to be a turning point in Hugh Stowell Brown's life is recorded in his *Commonplace Book* and can be dated to the late spring or early summer of 1876, perhaps a few weeks after the comments quoted above about his hard-working Sunday. For the first time in his life, Brown knew poor health. He succumbed to an episode of bronchitis and what he called 'congestion of the lungs and liver'. This was a time of serious illness in Liverpool. Liverpool had always been an unhealthy town, although it had worked hard to counter the worst illnesses that affected such a poor and overcrowded place. The appointment of Dr William Duncan as the town's Medical Officer of Health in 1847 was the first such appointment in Britain, and he had seen how diseases of the lung had been a persistent problem in the town. In May 1876 the town mayor, Peter Thompson, had died in office from an illness of the lungs, the chairman of the Dock Board had died in the same way, and now Brown had the same illness.

Brown was clearly shaken and frightened. He recorded not just the symptoms of his illness but his emotional distress and the effect the illness had on his faith. He went to the North Yorkshire spa town of Harrogate to recuperate and had plenty of time to think, perhaps for the first time for many years. He says that although his illness was very much like the mayor's, he was not worried. He records, 'I have a singular freedom from anxiety in the absence of all strong desires of any kind, except a thirst for good soda water.'

What does concern Brown at this time is that way the illness affects his faith. He says:

> When I was very low and weak I found Atheism rather a temptation, as affording me a lazy escape from all bother, and chiefly the bother of having to live for ever ... I find that sickness makes me selfish ... Religion is simply latent in me when I am not well.[32]

It was during his time in Harrogate that he also determined that he needed to work less hard. Instead of the braggadocio of how many hours he could work on a Sunday, illness was teaching him that he could not go on this way forever. Among the resolutions he makes to himself, he writes:

> I will not work as I have done, for my work, especially in pulpit preparation, has always been

[32] Ibid, p 198.

very severe. I will read more and talk less. I will resolutely refuse to preach on Sunday afternoons. These preachings, with their journeys, have been a great drain upon me. I will have nothing to do with special services and anniversary meetings. I will withdraw as much as I can from Societies and their talkee-talkee committees. I will try to keep my own vineyard better. Sermons shorter by five minutes would be an improvement; my preaching must be less commonplace, bolder and more in accordance to the free thought of the age and not mere platitudes of Evangelicalism.[33]

Then he comes to at least one decision that he carries though in the following year: 'I shall keep in view the appointment of an assistant to become, if all goes well, my successor.' It took another year for this to come about and the man who was appointed was never going to be Brown's successor, but he did press forward with the idea of sharing his work with another minister.

Calling for help

At the end of 1877, as Brown completed thirty years in the pastorate of Myrtle Street and as he approached an arduous year in which he was to serve as president of the Baptist Union, he proposed that the church should take on an assistant minister. Rev Henry Lapham, who had just completed his studies at Regent's Park College in London (now in Oxford), was appointed by the church to the role. Although the church could not have been lacking in funds,

---

[33] Ibid, p 198.

Lapham's stipend was paid wholly out of a reduction in Hugh Stowell Brown's stipend. Hugh records that he wanted an assistant to relieve the pressure of his work, and the reduction in his own stipend suggests that he was hoping for a reduction in his own workload.

Brown's proposal, outlined to the church meeting in December 1877, was for an assistant who would conduct the Sunday evening services and services at the mission stations. This is not at all in keeping with his own plan for 'apprenticeship' that he later outlined to the Baptist Union in his presidential address, but more like the intention he had formed during his convalescence in Harrogate. But having an assistant at Myrtle Street did not suit Brown at all.

Lapham began work at Myrtle Street on Wednesday 19th June 1878, and resigned on 19th July 1880, leaving the church that September. Brown speaks of Lapham very kindly. He says he was 'all I could desire as a gentleman, a friend and a pastor, and many of my Church and congregation agreed with me, and prized him and his work highly'. But after two years the 'experiment', as he calls it, was abandoned and Lapham left the church. Henry Lapham went on to serve with the Baptist Missionary Society in Ceylon (now Sri Lanka) with great distinction. His resignation led Hugh to consider retirement. In late August 1880, as Lapham was leaving, Hugh decided that the work was too much for him, as he would have to go back to doing it on his own, which he could not bear, and the only solution was to submit his own resignation to the church.

To go, or not to go?

Hugh didn't want to leave Liverpool. He wanted to make himself available to others, working for the Association and the Missionary Society, taking on the role of 'kindly oversight' of local churches. He was also considering going back to some Sunday afternoon public lectures, delivering, as he said, 'addresses of the old sort, quite free from dogma – humane, natural, having to do with daily life'. In the Preface to Brown's memoirs, William Caine records that when Brown resigned in 1880 he often said that would like to open a hall in Oxford or Cambridge where he could teach young men from Baptist and Independent churches, alongside the arts curriculum of the university. He was clearly frustrated with the weekly demands of the oversight of a large church, more than with his calling to be a minister of the gospel.

At the largest church meeting ever held at Myrtle Street on Monday 30th August 1880, Hugh told the church he would be resigning the pastorate, effective from the following March. He says he had talked over his decision with his closest confidant, Charles Birrell. Birrell had been pastor at Pembroke Chapel in Liverpool from 1838 to 1872 and was himself enjoying retirement, though by 1880 he was in poor health and died in December of that year. Brown said, according to the minutes of the meeting, he 'had given the subject long and prayerful consideration and his determination was unalterable'.

Deacon Edward Mounsey replied on behalf of the church members. He expressed the 'profound sorrow' of the meeting and its 'grateful recognition of the ministry which for upwards of thirty-two years has drawn together and built up the faith of our Lord Jesus Christ'. The meeting accepted the resignation and resolved that they would find another pastor for the church.

In the following weeks his announcement, Brown received a letter signed by no fewer than 1,000 people from the church asking him to reconsider his decision. At first Brown would not relent and the church started looking for a new minister. Rev Richard Glover from Bristol was approached but declined the offer.

In December 1880, while Brown was attending the funeral of his friend Charles Birrell, a church meeting proposed that another approach be made to Brown to reconsider 'on the understanding that a co-pastor be appointed as speedily as possible'. Despite his 'unalterable determination', Hugh agreed to this proposal.

So Myrtle Street began to find another minister to work alongside Hugh Stowell Brown. To take on such a task would be seen a privilege but also a burden, living in the shadow of a man with such a reputation. In January 1881 the church found the man willing to take on the job: a Mr Lewis from Rochdale who had recently preached at the church on a Sunday morning. But then Lewis changed his mind and declined the appointment, and no one else could be found to take the post. The man who, as its president, called on the Baptist Union to encourage churches such as Myrtle Street to take on ministerial apprentices was not able to find anyone to be his apprentice or his colleague. Was this a judgement on his personality, on his reputation, or the lack of available men?

Hugh concludes this episode in his memoirs by reflecting on the task he was called to continue:

At this time my health was exceptionally good, as if to fit me for the task of resuming the work as before, so I determined to thank God and take courage, and to struggle on with the work as He might give me strength, and to say nothing more about the question of resignation.[34]

Starting again

After Brown resumed his ministry, the leadership of the church was restructured in May 1881. Clearly leadership was an issue. The church had dismally failed to find anyone to be co-pastor alongside Brown in the church and more 'lay' leaders were needed. To compound the situation, in March of that year twenty-six members had been released to form the nucleus of the membership at Princes Gate Church and among them some gifted leaders. The solution was to appoint elders as well as deacons: to have no more than six additional deacons and no more than twelve elders, though the deacons would also be considered as elders ex officio. A meeting was held of male members only, and from these members the pastor and deacons were to suggest men suitable for the offices of deacon and elder. At the meeting six new deacons were elected and sixteen names were put forward for the role of elder, of whom twelve were elected.

Three days later there was a full church meeting where Brown explained to the church that the newly elected elders had 'mainly in their charge the visitation of the sick, those absent and in trouble, candidates for membership

---

[34] Ibid, p 125.

and new members'.[35] He suggested that this pattern of leadership was the one used at the Metropolitan Tabernacle – Spurgeon's church in London.

This reordering of leadership and the inclusion of more people in leadership roles was clearly a response to the inability of the church to find a pastor to work alongside Brown after his assistant Henry Lapham had left and Brown had tried to resign. In contemporary Church practice, the group that Myrtle Street elected as elders would more likely be referred to as 'pastoral visitors', and this shows how important this work of pastoral care was in the church. Even more strange to the modern sensibility is to have a meeting from which women are excluded, but this would not have been unusual in Victorian Britain, even in egalitarian Baptist churches.

The issue of members who did not attend worship was one that concerned the church, and with such a large membership it was difficult to monitor. A scheme was agreed in 1881 to issue communion tickets. Members would be issued with tickets which they had to give in at communion services. Members were expected to attend 'all the means of grace' including both Sunday services, the Lord's supper twice a month (first Sunday of the month in the morning, third in the evening), the prayer meeting on a Monday evening and the lecture on a Wednesday evening. They were also expected to 'use' the weekly offering boxes.

At a meeting the following year the scheme was reviewed, and it was agreed that the church would remove from membership anyone who has not attended a

---

[35] Minute-book of Myrtle Street Baptist Church, entry for May 1881.

communion service for twelve months and has been visited by the elders and has no 'reasonable excuse'. At the same meeting the pastor recorded an increase in membership, especially by baptism and more than ever before among young people, so it appeared that the crackdown on attendance had done no harm. Another year later it was reported that forty members had been removed from the roll for non-attendance at communion.

Each year at the annual meeting Sunday school figures were also reported: the number of teachers, the number of 'scholars' and the size of the library. These figures are difficult to monitor through the years because of branch churches and mission stations sometimes being included and sometimes dropping out of the statistics. To give a flavour of the numbers, in 1883, when the numbers at Myrtle Street reached their peak, and for the mother church alone, the Sunday school reported forty-nine teachers, of whom twenty-eight were men and twenty-one women. They had in their care 474 children – 228 boys and 246 girls – four more than the previous year – with an average weekly attendance of 330. The Sunday school library held 2,420 volumes and 112 readers.

By the time Brown died, the number of members at Myrtle Street chapel was 593 and, including the members of the mission stations and churches that were still part of Myrtle Street, the number was 960. This did not include churches that by then had their own membership rolls. Those numbers were only the members, not those who attended but had not formally become members, and it did not include the children. And that was just a snapshot in time, the final year of Brown's thirty-nine years of service at Myrtle Street. And he would be the first to say that numbers were just numbers: what mattered were the people that they represented – people whose lives had been changed and challenged and enriched by his work.

The pastorate of Myrtle Street chapel was, above all his other achievements, Hugh Stowell Brown's life's work. It was the work to which he gave most of his time and effort. He laboured for the best exposition of the Christian message he could give, and he laboured on behalf of people he cared for. He found church life frustrating and would have given up the committees and regulations and councils and structures in a moment, but he knew that part of the work had to be done for the gospel message to fly free and to reach the hearts of the people, for the transformation of the world. In the end, though, in my opinion, it was Myrtle Street chapel that killed him. When he died in post, it was largely because he had worked too hard for too long and when he had pleaded with the church to allow him to share the work, they had not responded, so he had laboured on alone until he had no more strength to give.

6

The Concert Hall Lectures

Of all Hugh Stowell Brown's activities and campaigns, the one that secured his reputation in Liverpool was his series of Sunday lectures in the Concert Hall. Every Sunday afternoon in the winter and spring from 1854 to 1861 Hugh delivered his 'Lectures to Working Men' to audiences of several thousand people

The Concert Hall

The hall was on the north side of Lord Nelson Street between Hotham Street and St Vincent Street, near Lime Street station. In the nineteenth century it was a popular venue for musical events as well as public lectures and housed a large upper hall and a smaller lower hall. In recent years the Concert Hall has been converted into flats, known as the Trafalgar Warehouse Apartments.

A major precursor to the Sunday afternoon lectures in Liverpool was a lecture delivered by Brown in October 1853. The contemporary artist Charles Lucy had produced an oil painting called *Departure of the Pilgrims from Delft Haven* in 1847. This won a prize at the Westminster Hall competition in London in 1847 and was exhibited at the Royal Academy in 1848. In 1853 the painting came to

Liverpool and was exhibited at the Gallery of Arts in Church Street.

The subject matter of the painting was a group of English Separatists praying together just before their departure from Holland for the New World. The central figure is their minister, John Robinson, leading them in prayer. The exhibition of this award-winning painting created interest in the work of art and in its subject matter. In a move that promoted both the art exhibition and the cause of the nonconformist churches of the town, it was decided to hold a public lecture on the subject of 'The Pilgrim Fathers'.

The venue was to be the Concert Hall in Lord Nelson Street and the lecturer was to be the esteemed Baptist preacher Hugh Stowell Brown. Hugh had just turned thirty years old and had only been in the town a few years, but his reputation was clearly already established. The report of the event reads: 'the well-known eloquence and great popularity of the lecturer drew together a large audience, the hall being crowded to excess sometime before the appointed hour.'[36]

The lecture was so popular that it was delivered twice, on both the Tuesday and the Thursday of the last week of October 1853. For the occasion the highly valuable painting was brought into the Concert Hall and suspended over the platform, illustrating the lecture. Brown's lecture was

---

[36] Introduction (anonymous) to Hugh Stowell Brown, *The Pilgrim Fathers: a lecture by the Rev. Hugh Stowell Brown, delivered October 25 & 27, 1853 illustrative of the government prize picture, by Charles Lucy, the Departure of the Pilgrim Fathers (A.D. 1620.)* (London: Thomas Agnew and Sons, 1854), p 5.

erudite and witty, taking the listener to the coastlands of the United States and Holland, to the privations of life in the seventeenth century and the glorious heritage of religious liberty. It reads like a rousing speech at a political conference. And it was received with applause and cheers throughout and with 'loud and long-continued cheering' as it ended.

This 'Pilgrim Fathers' lecture proved that Hugh Stowell Brown could stir a crowd outside his church and that people would come the Concert Hall to hear him. It was the seedbed of a series of lectures that were to follow.

Through the 1850s there was a growing trend across the country for nonconformist churches to reach out to people who wouldn't or couldn't attend church services by taking church into public halls. These became known as 'theatre services' because they were often held in the local theatre, a place then considered out of bounds for good God-fearing people. One well-known lecturer was the Baptist minister Rev Arthur Mursell, who gave several series of lectures in Birmingham, and then in Manchester.

An article in the Baptist weekly *The Freeman* in 1856 encouraged churches to go to people rather than expecting the people to go to church, and recommended theatre services as an idea. Halls such as the Free Trade Hall in Manchester and the Temperance Hall in Bradford were used for Christian outreach events, and the first theatre service in London was held in 1859 in Hoxton. But, before all these, the Liverpool series run by Myrtle Street chapel were the first of their kind anywhere in the country. They were founded not by Brown but by his friend and church member Nathaniel Caine.

Nathaniel Caine was a significant industrialist of his day. He owned several mining companies in Barrow-in-Furness and in Millom in Cumberland. His father was a Manxman who had moved to Liverpool to pursue his business. Nathaniel Caine had been a Wesleyan Methodist, but, unusually for the time, when he married he joined the church where his wife was a member, Myrtle Street Baptist. He remained a member of and a generous contributor to Myrtle Street for the rest of his life and served for many years as a deacon, a lay leader, of the church.

Caine was a philanthropist who paid much of the cost of the building of Abbey Road Baptist Church in Barrow-in-Furness and the entire cost of the building of a Wesleyan chapel in Broughton-in-Furness, as well as the Temperance Hall in Broughton, built for the workers at his Hodbarrow iron mine in Millom. Nathaniel Caine was the father of William Sproston Caine, who was a leading Liberal politician of his day and married Hugh's daughter, Alice. Nathaniel Caine's daughter, Phoebe, was also Hugh's second wife.

The first lectures

Caine hired the Concert Hall on Saturday evenings to run a series of free concerts for the poorer people of the town in an attempt to offer an alternative to the many pubs and alehouses of Liverpool. Working with Mr J Calderwood, editor of the *Liverpool Mercury*, Caine booked the best-known local singers of his day to perform and usually presided over the concerts himself. Over the stage he put up the motto 'to make the man a better mechanic, and the mechanic a better man'.

Based on the success of the Saturday evening concerts, on 1st May 1854, Nathaniel Caine initiated a series of Sunday afternoon lectures for people who seldom went to church. Many people in Liverpool in the mid-nineteenth century lived in great poverty and even those who didn't experience the worst of the town's slums wouldn't have been able to dress up in the 'Sunday clothes' that were thought to be necessary to attend church. So Caine decided he would take church to the people, in a context where best clothes were not needed. The idea was right for its time and started a movement that would survive into the twentieth century. Writing in 1905, Alexander Maclaren of Manchester credited these Sunday afternoon lectures with the rise of what later in the century was known as the PSA, the 'Pleasant Sunday Afternoon' movement.

A growing attraction

The first few lectures were to be delivered by Caine's minister, Hugh Stowell Brown, and were held in the lower room, the smaller of the two rooms in the Concert Hall. About 200 attended. Brown spoke, after a short introduction from Caine, 'of the Great Teacher and what he taught'. Other eminent nonconformist preachers took their turn in that first series, but the one the public loved to hear was Hugh Stowell Brown. As spring turned to summer the weather got warmer and the crowds grew larger, and the lectures moved upstairs to the large hall. Within a few months, the attendance had reached 1,500. By

Hugh Stowell Brown, 1859 (photo: public domain)

the time the second series of lectures began, the speaker was the same every week and the lectures became not Caine's but Brown's, with different people introducing the speaker each week.

On an anniversary of the lecture series later in his life, Brown wrote of his aims in the lectures. He said:

> I have always had at heart the welfare of the working men, and I have felt that in addressing them it is necessary to be as free as possible from all conventional phraseology current among sects and Churches. I take you to witness that I have never used my position here for the purpose of

proselytising any man for the purpose of making him a Baptist or a Dissenter. I have tried to win you over to Christ, to induce you to lead sober, righteous, and godly lives.[37]

A number of contemporary accounts of the lectures exist, as well as the text of sixty-three published lectures and the titles of another four. The *Liverpool Mercury* of Monday 23rd November 1857 gives us an account of the previous day's lecture, 'Five Shillings and Costs'. It describes how 'an immense audience' was in attendance that Sunday, the same as every Sunday, and that several thousand people were not able to get into the hall. So that more could hear the lecture, the lower hall was used as an overspill, and while Brown spoke in the upper hall, a Mr Calderwood read the same lecture in the lower hall. Right through to the end of the lecture the street outside the hall remained crowded with people who still hoped to get in, but they could not. The *Mercury* article says that 4,000 did manage to hear the lecture, but that 'a room capable of holding 7,000 or 8,000 would have been crammed'. It also notes that 'it was satisfactory to find that a very large proportion of the persons who attended belong to the working classes'.[38] Brown had been asked to deliver the lectures twice in the afternoon but he said that as he had to preach at his church in the evening and then in Bristol on the Monday and in London on the Tuesday, he did not have the strength.

---

[37] Hugh Stowell Brown, quoted in John C Carlile, *The Story of the English Baptists* (London: James Clarke & Co, 1905), p 266.
[38] *Liverpool Mercury*, 23rd November 1857.

This one snapshot of Lord Nelson Street on a Sunday afternoon is an insight into the immense following of the lectures and Brown's own personal magnetism. It also reminds us of the demands that his celebrity brought. He was always travelling somewhere, speaking all over the country, and yet committed to being in Liverpool on Sundays to preach twice at Myrtle Street and to lecture at the Concert Hall. He also felt the weight of the responsibility of delivering a message to so many people. In the days before radio and television, very few people were heard by so many listeners, and with such popularity came the burden of knowing the significance of every word he spoke.

The London newspaper *The Illustrated News of the World* in its edition of 14th August 1858 published a picture of Myrtle Street chapel with the caption: 'The Rev. Hugh Stowell Brown's Chapel, Liverpool'. The text accompanying the picture, though, was not about the chapel but about Brown's Sunday afternoon lectures. The piece said:

> In addition to the usual services in the chapel, Mr Brown also lectures with great tact and no small success to the working men on Sunday afternoons. On these occasions he usually prefers the Concert-hall or some other building not specially set apart for public worship. The audiences are composed almost exclusively of men, the women not averaging more than five per cent. Of artisans and skilled workmen there are usually about sixty per cent, the remainder of the congregation consisting of unskilled labourers and young men in different offices and shops in the

town. These audiences number from two to three thousand, and from among them there are not a few who become regular attendants at the stated morning and evening services held in the chapel.[39]

Brown's lectures were quickly published and sold in large numbers, both singly and in various collected editions. The lecture 'Five Shillings and Costs', speaking against drunkenness, was reported to have sold 45,000 copies. In 1859, a volume of Brown's Concert Hall lectures was published in the United States with the title *Lectures for the People*. The volume was issued by G G Evans of Philadelphia and edited by Dr R Shelton Mackenzie who wrote a long and flowery 'biographical introduction', introducing Hugh Stowell Brown to the readers of America. Among some inaccurate biographical information, Mackenzie, a literary critic, praises the literary merit of Brown's writing and has particular regard for his down-to-earth style born, he claims, from the fact that Brown himself was a working man, that, he says, 'he himself has actually belonged to and labored, with his own muscle and brain, among the very laboring classes whom he especially addresses'.[40]

Mixed reviews

An American review of Mackenzie's publication of the first volume of the lectures appeared in the *Presbyterian*

---

[39] The *Illustrated London News of the World*, 14th August 1858.
[40] R Shelton Mackenzie (ed), introduction to Hugh Stowell Brown, *Lectures for the People* (Philadelphia, PA: G G Evans, 1859).

Quarterly of October 1859 and was not highly impressed with his style. It reported:

> We cannot say that they strike us as remarkable, except for their straightforwardness and Saxon English. There is no genius like Ward Beecher's, and no wonderful humor and pathos like those of John R Gough. It is the plainest kind of talk, straight as an arrow at the head and heart – more the head, however – of his hearers, and we are very glad that they listen to it.[41]

A longer review of the Sunday afternoon lectures was included as an appendix to the longer version of Hugh's *Notes of My Life* in 1887. This was written by Henry Young, a friend to Hugh and to William Caine, who owned a publishing and bookselling company in South Castle Street.

Young tells how a full hour and a half before the planned start time of quarter past three the doors of the Concert Hall are open and people are taking their seats. Copies of previous lectures are on sale at the door. By half past two the building is full. Young describes the people he observes in the hall: nearly all working class, all decently dressed. There are men and women of all ages, and children, and as they wait for the meeting to start they are reading books and magazines.

At ten past three Hugh Stowell Brown arrives at the hall by carriage and steps on to the platform as people wait in silence for him to begin. Young describes his delivery: he reads the lecture without any movement of his body, but

---

[41] *Presbyterian Quarterly*, October 1859.

he uses his voice emphatically to exhort and persuade his listeners of his points. He uses humour as well, which is met by general laughter, and the lecturer himself joins in the laughter.

Young comments on the advertised title of the talks as 'Lectures to the Men of Liverpool'. He says they are called lectures because, although they are Christian in content, the talks deal with the ordinary things of life. They are to 'men' not because women are excluded but because Brown can speak freely and frankly on topics that would not normally be spoken about with women present at that time. The word 'men' also implies that the talks are for all men whatever their faith or background. The content of the lectures, according to Young, is based on everyday experiences and argued not just from the Bible but from texts as diverse as Aesop's Fables and the writings of Benjamin Franklin.

Young comments on the literary character of the lectures and says they are 'easy reading', using straightforward language, without any complicated or difficult arguments. He says that some people have criticised the lectures for having no new ideas, only old truisms repackaged. Young says that if this is true, then that is the strength of the lectures – they are timeless truth simply told. Young says that Brown has an 'immense capacity for small things',[42] displaying an awareness of what we would call 'popular culture' such as the major and

---

[42] Henry Young 'Hugh Stowell Brown as Lecturer to Liverpool Working Men, from Notes by Henry Young', in ed W S Caine, *Extracts from His Commonplace Book*, in *Hugh Stowell Brown, A Memorial Volume*, p 532.

trivial stories reported in the newspapers and in the satirical magazine *Punch*. Young is impressed that Brown has read not just books by Christian writers but also works on contemporary concerns, such as the rise of advertising. He adapts a quotation by Francis Bacon to say that this kind of reading in popular culture and mixing with working people has made Brown 'a ready man' as well as a 'full man'. Brown is a 'ready man' in having so much information at his fingertips which he is able to draw upon and apply to everyday situations.

In the end, Young concludes, the evidence is in the crowds of people who come to hear the lectures. While other clergymen complain that they can't reach working-class men, Brown draws crowds of more than 2,000, and many of these are drawn to attend church as well.

For the people

The titles of the lectures give some indication of their approach to down-to-earth practical answers to the problems of everyday life. Titles such as 'Penny Wise and Pound Foolish', 'The Road to Hell is Paved with Good Intentions', 'I Can't Afford It' and 'Cleanliness Is Next to Godliness' illustrate the commonplace approach to practical living in the lectures.

A review of Brown's published work appeared in *The Spectator* after his death in 1887 and was rather sniffy about the populist titles and language of Brown's lectures. The unnamed reviewer wrote:

> We can readily believe that, animated by the living voice of a strong and earnest preacher, such as Mr.

Brown, they would have the ring of true eloquence. But he was not above having recourse to the clap-trap titles which draw uncultivated audiences – and which have, therefore, their uses, – such as we find at the head of many of his very telling concert hall lectures on Sunday afternoons, — 'Stop Thief!' 'I don't care,' 'Keep to the Right,' 'The Devil's Meal is all Bran,' &c.[43]

The content of the lectures was practical and down to earth, with frequent contemporary references. His most talked-about lecture was one about 'Palmer the Poisoner', delivered in June 1856. This lecture, trailed well in advance, aroused so much interest that it was delivered twice on the one day, first in a theatre in Parliament Street in the early afternoon and then at the regular time at the Concert Hall. The subject of the lecture was William Palmer, the 'Rugeley Poisoner', whom Charles Dickens called 'the greatest villain that ever stood in the Old Bailey'.[44] Palmer had been hanged for the murder of his friend and was suspected of poisoning several others, including his brother.

The lectures covered subjects that mattered to people: money, debt and finances; housing and social conditions; drinking and over-indulgence; relationships in the family and between the social classes. Every lecture has reference to contemporary and popular affairs, and every lecture has

---

[43] *The Spectator*, 30th April 1887, p 21.

[44] Charles Dickens, 'The Demeanour of Murderers', *Household Words*, Saturday 14th June 1856, p 1.

reference to the Christian gospel and the message of Christ, without ever getting 'preachy' or pious.

One example of a typical lecture will need to suffice here to give a flavour of what his style and his content was like. We shall take as the example the lecture 'Penny Wise and Pound Foolish' which appeared as Lecture Seven in Mackenzie's edition of *Lectures for the People*.[45] The full corrected text of this lecture can be found as an appendix to this volume.

Penny wise and pound foolish

The lecture amounts to 5,440 words, which would take about forty minutes to read out loud at a medium pace and uninterrupted. The lecturer would have been introduced by Nathaniel Caine, and the lecture begins with no pleasantries, no reference to the previous week or extraneous words, but straight into the subject matter, the title of which would have been advertised in advance. The opening statement, 'There is in the world a good deal of false economy, which turns out in the end to be great and ruinous extravagance', is a fine summary of what is to come but does demand the listener gives the lecturer their full attention from the very beginning.

The lectures often use well-known sayings and proverbs, both biblical and otherwise, and this lecture has four of them in the first paragraph to illustrate the subject of this lecture. The one he settles on is the lecture's title – 'penny wise and pound foolish'. This saying, which is now

[45] Hugh Stowell Brown, ed R Shelton Mackenzie, *Lectures for the People*, pp 137-146.

out of use, was used in English as long ago as the sixteenth century and was clearly well known in Brown's day.

After a brief foray into an issue of public policy – the great number of alcohol licences being issued – the lecture has five areas in which it illustrates poor financial management at different levels of society. But choosing an issue that relates to people in different economic situations, the lecture is designed to speak to all his listeners and readers and to suggest that good household management is possible at all levels of society.

Firstly, he speaks to parents, particularly to parents who have boys in school. He urges parents to keep boys in school beyond the age at which they might earn some money, maybe the age of twelve. Instead, he urges, a boy should remain in school up to the age of fifteen, so he may have better prospects in later life. His reference is to boys because very few girls in poorer families were schooled in the 1850s. This was before the Elementary Education Acts of 1870 and 1880 insisted on compulsory attendance at school for boys and girls up to the age of ten, and later in 1899 the school-leaving age was raised to only twelve years of age. Most children who were in school in the 1850s were in elementary day schools run by the churches and the large majority were under the age of twelve. For a boy to remain at school until the age of fifteen would require a family to have sufficient wealth and for there to be available schools. For Brown, saving money by ending education was a false economy because a poorly educated population would remain poor.

His second subject where false economies can be made is a subject he speaks of more than any other in the lectures:

the housing of the poor. The living conditions of the poor in central Liverpool in the middle of the century were appalling and degrading. The Irish famine had led to immigration from Ireland and a sudden increase in the town's population. Over 90,000 people entered the town in the first three months of 1846 alone. In addition, industrialisation had brought a steady flow of people in from the countryside and had seen the town's population boom with a resultant overcrowding. Brown says in his lecture that it is a false economy, 'penny wise and pound foolish', to 'crowd the largest number of human beings into the smallest possible space'. He calls the housing 'abominable kennels' and the 'haunts of pestilence and death'. In the lecture the fault for this is shared. Some of the blame lies with the municipal and health authorities who do not work hard enough to provide good housing. Some fault lies with those who advertise poor housing as good, and some lies with those among the poor who don't care for their housing. He says there are 'many whose love of dirt leads them to prefer these tumble-down hovels'.

The solution, he says, is for the working man to spend as much of his wage as possible on getting a home far away from the worst housing and move into better surroundings. This will improve his life and his health and even his morals. He says:

> I do not say that if the wretched, drunken, dissolute inhabitants of some of our courts and alleys could be transported to some district containing well-built, airy, cheerful, healthy houses, they would be altogether converted by the change, but I do believe that they would be very greatly altered for the better

– that they would become more susceptible of good impressions – that they would be far more likely to become virtuous and godly people, more likely to listen to the Gospel, and more likely to live the Gospel; certainly their bodily health would be improved, their lives would be lengthened, their children's morals would not be so exposed to corrupting influences; and, altogether, I do most thoroughly believe that good dwellings would go very far towards improving the character and condition of the people in almost every respect.[46]

This seems to be the weakest part of the lecture and the passage least sympathetic to the plight of those caught up in genuine poverty, whose efforts to get out of poverty are only exacerbated by the poverty of their housing.

This section of the lecture also contains the section with the lightest touch and the most humour. He gives a mock advertisement of how an estate agent should advertise a property for the poor if it were to be honest and truthful. It is 'The house is largely stocked with various kinds of vermin, and the neighbourhood is celebrated for its bad smells and stagnant gutters', it says, and promises the new householder 'two man-fights and five woman-fights every week'. It is also a no-go area for the police, but awash with gin shops and pawnbrokers. In this section Brown is at his most witty and inventive, but also biting and satirical, worthy of space in *Punch* magazine or Dickens' *Household Words*.

---

[46] Ibid, p 138.

The third subject of false economy in the lecture is aimed at those who spend their money unwisely on cheap goods, looking for great bargains, and end up with shoddy items which are not worth the money that is spent on them. Again we have a humorous illustration, that of a gentleman who bought a cheap suit which fell apart the first time he wore it so that he had to retreat to his lodging in rags. This section is presumably aimed at the *nouveau riche*, those who were starting to get more prosperous in the booming town of Liverpool and had new decisions to make as to how to spend their wealth. Brown himself would have been counted among this number and was now earning far more than he has previously received as an engineer and far more than the salary that his father had enjoyed.

The fourth area of being 'penny wise and pound foolish' was in the salaries paid to servants. Many middle-class people had household servants at this time. In the 1851 census the Browns were a family of four living with two female servants or housemaids. In this section Brown encourages people who employ servants to pay them good wages. It is false economy, he argues, to pay servants as little as possible, because this will make them discontented and possibly dishonest.

Brown's final example of 'penny wise and pound foolish' behaviour is the pay-off that he has been heading towards throughout the lecture. Up to now this preacher has not quoted from the Bible or brought any distinctively Christian teaching. But now he speaks of the man who has 'neglected his soul' and now he quotes directly from the words of Jesus, from Luke 12:16-21, though he does not give chapter and verse. For Brown it is a matter of logical sense – the eternal soul must be of greater worth than any earthly riches, and he contends that this point does not need to be argued for it is clear to everyone except the 'infidel', who he considers to be the only person who would not believe in the coming judgement.

The lecture ends with a summary of the ground he has covered – a reminder of each of his main points and then a final appeal to the heart: 'may we shun that penny wisdom and pound folly, that minimum of wisdom and maximum of folly, which prefers sin to holiness, time to eternity, earth to heaven, and the body to the soul'.

Lecture or sermon?

The lectures were delivered on Sundays in public halls. Are they sermons in disguise? In the end it is a matter of semantics. Brown's lectures do not start from Bible texts the way his sermons do, and they are not full of biblical allusions. But like sermons they speak to the heart as well as to the will, and they are thoroughly biblical in their content and intent. They are clearly of their time and for a particular audience, but they are in their way a masterclass in Christian communication. The language is clear and direct and has a liberal use of humour. It is no wonder that the crowds came flocking to hear him week after week.

The Sunday afternoon lectures at Lord Nelson Street continued in their weekly format until 1861. This seven-year period was a period of intense activity for Brown, which included major building work on the Myrtle Street chapel and new initiatives in public life.

In his memoirs Brown records that the response received wasn't always favourable. He says that 'many were the letters I received about these lectures; some of them compliments, more of complaint, some thanking me, many growling at me and abusing me',[47] and that 'some thought there was no gospel in my lectures; others that there was too much'.[48] It is clear that although Brown loved to speak to large crowds, he didn't enjoy the public attention that the lectures brought to him. One result was that many people wrote to him begging for money.

The lectures also proved to be a strain on Brown as he was still expected to preach both morning and evening at Myrtle Street, even when he had such an impact on the wider community in the afternoons. The church work was, after all, what he was paid for, and that was what the church expected of him first and foremost. He writes that one correspondent did not believe that he did not have the time for the Sunday afternoon lectures; it was rather, the correspondent suggested, that 'I had nothing else to do and I had got tired because people did not pay for admission. I was just like other hirelings.'[49] It clearly hurt that some people thought that he was only doing it for the money, and giving up because there was not enough money in it for him.

---

[47] Hugh Stowell Brown, ed W S Caine, *Extracts from His Commonplace Book*, in *Hugh Stowell Brown, A Memorial Volume*, p 88.
[48] Ibid, p 88.
[49] Ibid, p 88.

Summer season

From 1855, the Concert Hall lectures were held in the winter and spring months, and after they ended Brown started a summer series of open-air lectures on Sunday evenings after the evening services at Myrtle Street. These attracted crowds of up to 4,000 people. To speak to a crowd of 2,000 in a hall and to be heard by every person is a feat in itself, but to speak to 4,000 people outdoors and for them to hear the preacher is remarkable.

Brown's reflections, later in life, on his public lectures, are quite poignant. He suggests that he has had a change of mind about the value of the lectures that took up so much of his time and energies in the prime of his life. He writes:

> My opinions in regard to such services have undergone a considerable change. I do think it far better that the rich and poor should meet together in the House of the Lord, than that we should even seem to encourage their separation by holding special services for the working men in halls, theatres and the like. What I am much more desirous of effecting is this – to offer every encouragement and facility for the attendance of all classes at our places of worship, to adapt our services to working men in so far as they need such adaptation, and to lead them to feel they really are all welcome in God's House.[50]

---

[50] Ibid, p 90.

The lectures encouraged working-class people to attend the Concert Hall on Sunday afternoons, but they were still not attending the chapel on Sunday mornings or evenings. There remained a separation of the richer, more educated people who felt more comfortable in church, and the less educated who felt more comfortable in a concert hall. Some people would consider that this did not matter, but clearly Hugh had a high view of the importance of the gathered community and of the place of worship, what he called 'God's House'. His vision is for the churches to be filled with people of all classes, not half-filled with the rich while the halls are filled with the 'working people'.

In churches to this day similar discussions continue. Should the mission of the church be adapted to aim different approaches to suit different people? Should we put on meetings just for young people, or just for women, or just for business people? Or is it more important to keep the unity of the church and hold all people together as one? These questions are as familiar to churches today as they were to Hugh Stowell Brown.

But, despite his change of heart, surely his years of time and energy in the lecture halls and the public squares were not wasted. Many people were moved to change their lives because of what they had heard, and wouldn't have arrived early and queued for a seat if the talks did not matter to them. The Concert Hall lectures built Brown's reputation outside the church. The printed versions of the lectures sold up to 10,000 copies. And 150 years later Brown is still chiefly remembered for his Concert Hall lectures.

7
Public Life

Hugh Stowell Brown developed his ministry from being a local church pastor and a good sound preacher to becoming a man renowned in Liverpool and beyond, and from being a man tied to church affairs to being a man involved in the business of everyday life, especially the lives of the working people.

He travelled extensively throughout the British Isles: he knew the whole of Scotland and the whole of Ireland as well as England and Wales and made occasional return visits to the Isle of Man. William Caine wrote of Brown after his death:

> I do not think any minister in the Baptist denomination has filled so many pulpits as Hugh Stowell Brown. Possessed of an iron constitution, and what was more important, a church willing he should go, he was always ready to travel to Scotland, or Devonshire, or South Wales, to preach for some poor Church, or lecture in aid of some useful society.[51]

Brown's *Commonplace Book* is full of accounts of his visits to various towns across the British Isles, a large proportion

---

[51] W S Caine, *Preface to Hugh Stowell Brown, A Memorial Volume*, p xv.

of them in Scotland, where he was particularly drawn to the Free Church of Scotland. He also records speaking to Methodist groups, whom he always congratulates in their organisational skills, and to groups of General Baptists, where he felt welcomed but did not always appreciate the standard of their preaching.

The travelling preacher

Brown took holidays from the church, and spent most of them travelling, and wherever he travelled he preached at a church, or occasionally listened to the preaching of someone else, usually with a critical ear. As one example, Brown records a visit to Scotland in late 1875 where he was not impressed with what he witnesses on a casual visit to a church:

> One day in the month of December I had an hour to spare in Edinburgh, so went to the united daily prayer meeting in the Free Church Assembly hall. There were about four hundred present, seven-eighths of them women. Dr. H. B___ preached. I think I never was at so dreary a meeting. Every word was uttered in the most melancholy whining tone. There were many supplications for backsliders; so marked a feature was this as to suggest that the recent Moody and Sankey excitement had been followed by a dismal reaction.[52]

---

[52] Hugh Stowell Brown, ed W S Caine, *Extracts from His Commonplace Book*, in *Hugh Stowell Brown, A Memorial Volume*, pp 150-151.

Whatever his attitude to others, Brown seems to have received a positive response to his preaching wherever he went. He clearly enjoyed the opportunity to spread his wings beyond the weekly task of preaching at Myrtle Street twice every Sunday and once in the midweek.

Scholarly lectures

Brown was in demand not just as a Sunday preacher but also as a lecturer. He was known for his popular lectures to the 'working men of Liverpool' and he often toured these lectures. But he also delivered some more serious and academic lectures that reveals the depth of his learning and education. Brown continued to study Church history and some of his public lectures demonstrate his erudition and depth of knowledge on theological matters.

In 1851, when Brown was aged just twenty-seven and had been at Myrtle Street for three years, he was invited to be one of the contributors to a series of lectures in Liverpool from January to April organised by the Liverpool Sunday School Institute. The institute was an august body made up of Sunday school teachers which boasted an impressive historical and theological library, which was later commended by Bishop J C Ryle. Its lecture series for 1851 was to be 'Eight Lectures on the Great Protestant Reformers', and was presided over by Dr William Hendry Stowell, the Congregational minister and president of Cheshunt College, who was a good friend to Hugh Stowell Brown. Hendry Stowell, as he was known, was, like all the Stowells, a Manxman – the son of the William Stowell who was one of Hugh's teachers in

Douglas and the first Dissenter Hugh had encountered. He was not, however, Hugh's cousin or close relative, as accounts of Brown's life have recorded.

Hugh was asked, or chose, to speak as part of the lecture series on 'John Huss and Jerome of Prague'. These are not the best known of the early protagonists in the story of the Protestant Reformation but Hugh delivered a lecture of academic complexity and brilliance. The language is rather flowery and overblown, characteristic of his early preaching style, and suggests that he laboured over it for a long time. But its scholarship is immense, beginning with an account of how the Slavs became Catholic and then the influence of Wycliffe on Huss, and the lives and work of Huss and Jerome. Brown is generous in his praise of the Moravian Brothers, whom he calls 'a denomination noted above all others for zeal – the first to translate the Bible into a European vernacular language – the first to send missionaries to heathen nations'.[53]

He is keen to remind his listeners that 'the work of the Reformers is not lost'. Just as a drop of water cannot be lost but is used elsewhere for another purpose:

> nor is one deed of righteousness that ever was performed, one word of truth that ever was proclaimed, one prayer of faith that ever presented by those illustrious martyrs lost to the world; for the deeds, the words, the prayers of the people of God are lasting as the elements of the material globe: yes, when these shall have perished from the spaces of

[53] Hugh Stowell Brown, 'John Huss and Jerome of Prague' in *Course of Eight Lectures on the Great Protestant Reformers by Various Ministers of the Liverpool Sunday School Institute* (London: Johnstone and Hunter, 1851).

creation, those will remain imperishable for ever and ever![54]

The language may be overblown, perhaps intended to impress his senior friends such as Hendry Stowell and Charles Birrell, who delivered a more measured lecture on Luther, but the scholarship was sound and impressive.

Throughout his life Brown was able to speak on subjects that demonstrated his breadth and depth of knowledge. In a lecture called 'A Commentary on Liverpool Life', which is undated but written in about 1856, Brown gives an erudite history of the town of Liverpool, starting with the castle built by King John and continuing to the development of the docks in the eighteenth century and into his own time. He gives a thorough analysis of the condition of the town drawn from the latest data from 1851, including demographics, migration records, church attendance, businesses and medical statistics.

He goes on to speak of aspects of the life of Liverpool which appear in the guide books alongside parts of the life of the town which would never make the pages of tourist manuals. He makes suggestions for the reform of the town: the reform of the system and the reform of morals. What is striking is that we see a passionate lecturer who is not just an idealist but a man who knows his subject, a man of learning and political astuteness who has researched his areas of interest and applied his intellect as well as his religious fervour to his subject.

One more example of his lectures will illustrate Brown's depth of knowledge. In 1873 Brown delivered a lecture in

---

[54] Ibid.

London entitled 'Is the Established Church the Bulwark of Our Protestantism?', in which he sketched out the history of the Protestant movement from the Diet of Spires (now usually called the Diet of Speyer) of 1529, taking in the work of Luther, Calvin, Cranmer, Ridley and Latimer and the various streams within the Church of England. It is a lecture that is sharp and polemical and historically sound.

Brown was also a man who laboured long and hard on practical concerns. He never simply lectured or preached about the things that mattered to him. He got involved and saw Christian faith as a practical matter: religion was belief with its sleeves rolled up, doing what you said you believed.

Offending the Manxmen

Brown was one of the founding members of the Liverpool Manx Society, a group designed to celebrate the culture of the Isle of Man and its people, but at its opening meeting he managed to upset a number of its founder members. The Liverpool Manx Society was founded at a meeting on 17th July 1876 and William Corlett was elected its first chairman. Its inaugural event was a tea party and concert on 25th November of that year at the Concert Hall on Lord Nelson Street. This hall, it was noted, had been built through the work of the Manxman Nathaniel Caine, a member at Myrtle Street chapel and father of William Caine and Hugh's second wife, Phoebe.

After the concert Hugh Stowell Brown was invited to speak. Now aged fifty-three, he was a high-profile public figure and an acclaimed public speaker with an impeccable

Hugh Stowell Brown's *carte de visite* (calling card)
(photo: Rev Dr David Steers, velvethummingbee.wordpress.com, used
by permission)

Manx pedigree. But what he said did not please his
audience. In the context of the meeting it can be supposed
that the audience were expecting a short witty paean of
praise to the Isle of Man and all it stood for and the
contribution its people had made to Liverpool. Instead he
chose to deliver a speech that was seen as critical of the
Island and its backward ways.

Writing on the death of the Manxman Thomas Callow in 1907 in *The Manx Quarterly*, an anonymous correspondent remembers it in this way:

> The Rev Hugh Stowell Brown, who made a clever and characteristic speech which caused quite a flutter in the dovecotes and created a mild sensation for at, [sic] the time it was looked upon as a wholesale denouncement of everything Manx, whereas, in the opinion of the writer (who took an active part in the proceedings of the evening), it was merely a splendid compliment to the thrifty plodding Manx character, and an idealistic endeavour to show how primitive were the conditions of things in Manxland. However it may have been read, or in whatever way it may have been interpreted, there is not the slightest doubt that the celebrated preacher may have been actuated by the same desire as was his Royal Highness the Prince of Wales when, on his recent return from his Colonial trip he uttered this memorable advice 'Wake up, Englishmen!' And the only fair interpretation that could be placed on the remarks of the gifted speaker was that they were intended to convey to his listeners how truly primitive were the conditions of things Manx, and his earnest desire that Manx people should be abreast of things in the present-day go-aheadedness, or, in other words, 'Wake up, Manxmen!'[55]

---

[55] Anonymous obituary, *The Manx Quarterly*, no 1, February 1907, p 28.

The text of the speech Brown gave that day shows it to be an honest account of his poor childhood, a speech written for an audience who would take for granted their affection for the Island and their loyalty to it, but would not be unwilling to see the faults in their homeland. This was a speech more like his presidential addresses to the Baptist Union – a speech written for insiders who were willing to receive some criticism of their own society outside the public gaze. He does say, 'I have been in very many towns, but meaner, dirtier, nastier towns than Douglas, Castletown, Ramsey, and Peel, I do not remember,' but he manages to say it with great affection. The contemporary accounts of the speech record it being met with some disapproval but mainly with loud applause.

Another Manxman, S K Broadbent (possibly the same writer as the above correspondent), speaking to the Douglas Progressive Debating Society in February 1908, remembered that speech in this way:

> It was at one of the great Manx meetings that he [Brown] delivered a remarkable speech, which caused great offence to his countrymen. They did not see it at first – they rather enjoyed his good-humoured sallies; but when they saw it in cold type, and read it again and again, they were greatly incensed. And to the eternal shame of Manx people, they never forgave him, I confess I see nothing to offend anyone, it was meant to take his countrymen

down a peg or two, but surely it was not an unpardonable offence.[56]

Writing in 1909 Ralph Hall Caine, another Liverpool Manxman, recorded in his brief sketch of the life of Hugh Stowell Brown, 'Once Mr. Brown gave a Manx audience in Liverpool more keen thrusts than were either true or fair.'[57]

Broadbent's suggestion that the Manx people never forgave him must be seen as an exaggeration, and he was forgiven. In the notice of his death in the *Liverpool Echo* of 26th February 1886 it is reported, 'the Manx association will be represented to pay tribute to their distinguished fellow-countryman',[58] and at Brown's funeral the procession was led out from his home to the cemetery by representatives of the Manx community.

One other notable connection Brown must have made through the Liverpool Manx Society is with the solicitor William Quilliam, later Abdullah Quilliam. Quilliam was born in Liverpool in 1856 of Manx descent and had part of his education at King William's College on the Island, where Brown also studied. Quilliam qualified as a solicitor in 1878 and was a lifelong active member of the Liverpool Manx Society, serving as its chairman in 1906. Quilliam is remembered for his conversion to Islam and founding England's first mosque and Islamic centre at Brougham Terrace, Liverpool, in 1889. Although there is no record of a meeting between Quilliam and Brown it is more than likely that they knew each other as fellow temperance

---

[56] S K Broadbent, *The Manx Quarterly*, no 5, November 1908, p 404.

[57] W Ralph Hall Caine, *Isle of Man*, p 193.

[58] *Liverpool Echo*, 26th February 1886.

campaigners, and Quilliam may well have been present at Brown's lecture in 1876.

The Workman's Bank

The work that Hugh Stowell Brown considered his greatest achievement outside his Christian ministry of preaching and lecturing was the foundation of his Workman's Bank. In his *Notes of My Life* he devoted a short chapter to record the foundation and progress of this ground-breaking work. Writing in 1884, he recorded that the Workman's Bank had been founded by Myrtle Street chapel in 1861 and since that date 3,000 people had deposited money with the bank, adding up to a total of £80,000 of what he calls 'working people's money'.

The first 'savings bank' for working people had been opened in Ruthwell in Dumfries by Rev Henry Duncan in 1810. Duncan had worked in a bank in Liverpool for three years, before entering the ministry, where he had gained his knowledge of financial affairs. In Ruthwell, sixpence was all you needed to open an account, while the official banks required a £10 deposit to open an account.

In the same spirit, Brown pioneered the opening of the Myrtle Street Workman's Bank to allow the ordinary working people to save their money. A bank requires the confidence of its investors, and in the case of the Myrtle Street Workman's Bank that confidence was largely placed in Brown himself. He writes in his memoirs that 'it is a great satisfaction to me that we have so far secured the confidence of a very large number of working people'.[59]

He records only two minor 'runs' on the bank that resulted from the failures of commercial banks, to show the confidence the public had in his institution while other banks were failing. In 1866 Barned's Bank collapsed as a result of a national banking crisis, and one depositor in the Workman's Bank demanded the return of his ten shillings. In October 1867 the Royal Bank of Liverpool collapsed and Brown has his tongue firmly in his cheek as he records, 'we had to stand the rush upon us of another fifteen shillings'.[60] These, he said, were the only cases of any lack of confidence in his Workman's Bank during what he called 'the recent terrible times'.

The Myrtle Street Workman's Bank closed in the later years of Brown's life, not through any failure of the bank, but because its purpose was taken over by the public sector. In so many areas of public provision throughout British history, particularly health and education, the Church has led the way and the State has followed after, and this proved to be the case in the provision of saving facilities for the poorer people in British society. The facilities offered by the Workman's Bank were provided by the growth of the Post Office Savings Bank. The Post Office Savings Bank had been launched in 1861, the same year as Brown's Workman's Bank. The Palmerston government had seen it as a savings scheme to encourage ordinary wage earners to provide for themselves in hard times and

[59] Hugh Stowell Brown, ed W S Caine, *Notes of My Life*, in *Hugh Stowell Brown, A Memorial Volume*, p 92.
[60] Ibid.

illness. It began in a small way in London, but gradually spread. And, as it did, it took the place of the mainly church-led savings banks and led to the winding up of the Myrtle Street Bank.

For Hugh Stowell Brown the Workman's Bank always had first and foremost a moral purpose. It was not providing a social service, but a moral service, to improve the well-being of the people who mattered most to him: the working-class men and women of Liverpool. The bank gave the poor a stake in society and the means to save for long-term aspirations. It allowed wives to take their husbands' weekly pay packets and deposit the money safely out of harm's way where the money could not be wasted on alcohol. Brown saw this as the purpose of the bank. He wrote in his memoirs that 'the habits of saving which have thus been fostered, have been the salvation of hundreds from intemperance, from poverty, and from degradation'.[61] He chooses his words carefully: saving brings 'salvation' – a word with religious derivations. Brown's personal concerns about money, going way back to his own childhood, come to the fore again, and his concern for the alleviation of poverty is connected to temperance in all things and in a wholehearted commitment to Christian faith.

The Workman's Bank must also be seen in the context of the Sunday afternoon lectures. By 1861 Brown had a massive following among 'working men': many people who wouldn't usually go to church on a Sunday but were hungry to change their ways and to find a practical outworking of the moral agenda they were hearing in

---

[61] Ibid, p 91.

Brown's lectures. These were the people who joined his Workman's Bank. Brown makes the connection himself. He says:

> I think that in some measure, and a considerable measure, the working men, in so far as they have made this bank the depository of their savings, have done so through the knowledge of which they and I got of one another, and the good understanding established between us on those Sunday afternoons.[62]

In the first published volume of Brown's *Lectures to Working Men*, the first lecture in the collection is 'I Can't Afford It'. This wasn't the first lecture he ever gave, but it was one that was particularly well known. The lecture is not just about money: it is about a number of things we should say we 'cannot afford', such as 'losing time' and 'losing our good name', but it begins with a passage about the proper use of money. Brown is critical of those who spend money they can't afford in the gin shop or the beer shop, or on buying a new coat when the old one will suffice. He says: 'I think this is a good rule – that what we can't afford and well afford to pay for, we can't afford to have.'[63] Instead, he advises self-denial and managing without. The better alternative he puts forward in the lecture, and in all his teaching is developing 'the art of contentment'.

---

[62] Ibid.

[63] Hugh Stowell Brown, *Lectures to Working Men* (London: George Philip & Son, undated [about 1858]), p 7.

The Workman's Bank was significant because it summed up Brown's relationship with the working people of the town: people he sought to serve and to educate with that combination of a moral crusader and a political activist.

Missions, peace and politics

Brown was also involved in very many Christian causes and some that went beyond the Christian Church. He served on very many committees and gave his name and his time to countless charities. Closest to his heart were those groups which cared for the poor, especially the working poor, and those that offered practical solutions out of poverty.

Brown was a tireless supporter of the Baptist Missionary Society, the national agency by which British Baptists supported missionary work in other countries. This agency, currently known as BMS World Mission, has its roots in the work of William Carey, a Particular Baptist minister known as the father of modern missions. Through the work of Carey and Andrew Fuller, the Baptist Missionary Society was formed in 1792 and Carey was sent by the Society on its first mission to India.

Brown served on the national committee of the Baptist Missionary Society which meant long and tiring journeys to London, and he encouraged Myrtle Street to contribute to the funds of the Society, and they gave more than any other church in the country for many years.

Brown was a prominent member of the Liverpool Peace Society through all his years in the town to the end of his life and served as its president. The Society was a liberal and pacifist group which grew out of the London Peace Society and promoted a peacemaking approach to solving international disputes. Brown spoke at the Society's annual meetings on the incompatibility of Christianity and war, and the Society, under Brown's leadership, began a campaign of international disarmament and also campaigned against the death penalty.

Brown always said he was not interested in getting involved in politics, but in reality many political issues were part of his life. Like all the Baptists of his time, his politics were Liberal. Throughout his life he supported the Liberal Party in national and local politics and endorsed the Liverpool-born Liberal leader William Gladstone who was Prime Minister for four terms from 1868.

Brown was also a committed and prominent member of the Seamen's Friend Society. The Society, whose full name was the Liverpool Seamen's Friend Society and Bethel Union, was founded in 1820. It was the first charitable organisation in Liverpool formed to meet the needs of the many merchant seamen of the town and their families, and for people who gathered in Liverpool to sail to America and a new life in the New World. The Society opened the first floating chapel in Liverpool, it began a scheme of loaning books to ships, and towards the end of Brown's life in 1881 it opened a room in Mariners Parade as a reading room and sitting room for merchant seamen.

A different charity, the Mersey Mission to Seamen, was founded first in 1856 as a branch of the Mission to Seamen, and then re-established in 1873 as a more independent and autonomous organisation. Brown supported this work but was not directly involved in it. Brown also supported another group, the Royal Liverpool Seamen's Orphan Institution, which provided for the orphaned children of seamen and began its work in 1868.

Brown's support for charities connected with the sea continued to be a particular passion of his. Liverpool was a town built on its port and seafaring was the major source of its wealth. Although the last British slaver, the *Kitty's Amelia*, had left Liverpool under Captain Hugh Crow well before Brown's time in July 1807, and the trade was now abolished, Liverpool continued to profit from the trading connections which had been established by the slave trade.

In Brown's time Liverpool was still an expanding port town, the second port of the Empire, with strong trade links with India and the Far East and the Americas. Liverpool was also a major hub for the movement of people. There were always people passing through Liverpool: many on their way to America and many more fleeing from poverty in Ireland.

During the 1840s, many thousands of Irish migrants came into Liverpool, especially as a result of the Great Famine of 1845 to 1849. Almost 300,000 arrived in 1847 alone, and by 1851 about one-quarter of the population of the town had been born in Ireland.

But perhaps Brown had a more personal reason for supporting maritime charities. The sea was in his blood. As a Manxman, he knew the importance of the sea and he grew up watching the ships coming into Douglas harbour and playing around the shipyards. The earliest ancestor he knew about was a sea captain. More personally, Hugh's brother Robert had gone to sea and had died aged only twenty-six while he was far from home in the Bahamas. Hugh knew the privations and the challenges of the life of a merchant seaman and the debt that his family, and his adopted home of Liverpool, owed to such men.

The demon drink

The cause that was most important to Brown outside the simple gospel of Jesus Christ was the Temperance Movement. This was a cause that promoted a lifestyle without alcohol. Brown had some experience in his earlier working life of drinking alcohol. Just the once he had got drunk, when he had ended up in a ditch on that first working day in Biddulph. The experience had disgusted him and contributed to his opposition to drinking alcohol and the effect it had on people. This position was rooted in his concern for the poor and the way so much money was wasted in drunkenness. Although it was a stand he made as a Christian minister, it was more a moral stand than a religious one.

Brown's opposition to alcohol was also deep-rooted in his Manx background. He had grown up in the early days of the 'Independent Order of the Rechabites' on the Isle of Man and later identified himself as a Rechabite. The Rechabites began in Salford in 1835 and the Isle of Man was an early adopter of the cause in 1836, when Hugh was twelve years old. In December of that year the organisation voted to allow junior members under the age of sixteen, but it seems that Hugh didn't enrol at the time, although later in life he spoke at the Mona Union Tent, as their meetings were called.

Brown didn't wholeheartedly embrace the cause of Rechabitism and become a committed teetotaller until 1842, during his time in Wolverton. He records how he made that difficult decision in his *Notes of My Life*:

> About this time I became a teetotaler [sic] and a Rechabite, as did my fellow-lodgers. This brought me into great disfavour with the drinking workmen, and I was commonly called 'a __ teetotaler [sic].' The teetotalism led to my going to temperance meetings. The first in which I took part was held at the village of Daneshanger, where in attempting to make a speech I utterly broke down in confusion. Temperance meetings were scenes of great interruption and uproar: for attempting to persuade people to sobriety we were persecuted, hooted out of the villages, and pelted with mud.[64]

The village Brown calls Daneshanger, now called Deanshanger, is a four-mile walk from Wolverton, through Stony Stratford, across the Roman road of Watling Street and the River Ouse. It is noteworthy that Brown's first recorded public speech was defending his teetotalism and was a failure, and that he and his fellow abstainers were so badly treated in the workplace and in the general community.

In his time in Liverpool, Brown's teetotalism was reinforced by what he saw in the town: the number of places where strong drink was sold and consumed and the number of families who went hungry or lost their homes

---

[64] Hugh Stowell Brown, ed W S Caine, *Notes of My Life*, in *Hugh Stowell Brown, A Memorial Volume*, p 55.

because of it. He often spoke out against drunkenness and wasteful spending on drink. In his talks he was never adamant about his listeners becoming teetotal: he admitted that although he was an abstainer, a moderate amount of drink, within your budget, was not a sin. But to drink to excess so that you lost your power of reason, or to spend more than you could afford on drink, was an evil. And his target was never just the ale-drinking and gin-drinking working classes: he was equally critical of those middle-class drinkers who over-indulged themselves on spirits and port.

When Brown gave a lecture called 'A Commentary on "Liverpool Life"' in about 1856 he was scathing about the effect of the trade in alcohol. He noted that Liverpool had a population of 400,000 people, 165 places of worship and 2,341 public houses. This, he noted, amounted to '14 public houses for every church or chapel and one for every 94 of the adult population'.[65] He reckoned that every fifty men supported a single public house or beer house, but these places were 'frequented by as many women as men', and by children aged ten years and over. He claimed that one-third of those who were drunk and disorderly were under twenty-one years old. He had read that one publican could receive £14 in takings in one night, so the public houses were taking from the working people £82,000 per week, or four and a quarter million pounds each year.

Brown called for better regulation of the licensing system, and a strict enforcement of the withdrawal of licences from publicans who broke the laws, and he

---

[65] Hugh Stowell Brown, *A Commentary on 'Liverpool Life'*, a lecture by the *Rev Hugh Stowell Brown* (London: Gabriel Thompson, undated), p 3.

expressed his support for the movement towards earlier closing of licensed premises. But he also made positive suggestions for what he saw as more wholesome alternatives that the authorities should provide.

He suggested that Liverpool needed more parks and 'pleasure grounds', saying that as the town expanded it needed more 'lungs'. In this suggestion he was not alone, but he was ahead of his time. In the 1850s there were few public open spaces in Liverpool, but in the decades that followed many public parks were developed, most notably in this period Sefton Park, which was purchased for development as a public park in 1867.

Brown also suggested the establishment of a public gymnasium that would encourage young men to develop agility and strength and 'dissociate quoits, skittles and bowls from drinking'. In putting forward this suggestion it is likely that Brown knew of the work of John Hulley, known as 'the Gymnasiarch', and was of some influence on his life. Hulley was born in Liverpool in 1832. He was a champion gymnast and set up a gymnasium in Bold Street in Liverpool in 1858, just two years after Brown's influential speech on the need for such a facility, and then a second larger gymnasium in Myrtle Street, next to Myrtle Street chapel.

Hulley is now best known as one of the instigators of the modern Olympic movement. At his gymnasium he founded the National Olympian Association, and organised the first Grand Olympic Festival in Liverpool in 1862. Hulley died of a chest condition in 1875 and his funeral was conducted by Hugh Stowell Brown. At the funeral in Smithdown Road Cemetery on 11th January,

Brown spoke of the value of physical conditioning: 'exercises benefit the pupils in bodily health, but they led to the cultivation of manly habits, of temperance, and of self-denial, and so acted upon the moral character as well as the physical frame.'[66] In his *Commonplace Book* Hugh noted:

Today I buried John Hulley, the Gymnasiarch. He was at one time apparently a very popular man in Liverpool, but there were not more than a dozen people at his funeral. It is a heartless world![67]

In his campaign against alcohol, Brown was far from alone in Liverpool. He worked alongside fellow Dissenters, other Christians, and people who were not approaching the issue from a religious standpoint. One major comrade-in-arms in the Temperance Movement later in Brown's life was the influential Catholic priest Monsignor James Nugent. Father Nugent joined the temperance cause in the 1870s after a visit to America in 1870 which may have inspired Brown's later trip to the United States. According to his biographer, Nugent was urged by the Mayor of Indiana [*sic*] to become 'another Father Matthew',[68] to follow in the footsteps of Father Theobald Matthew, who had persuaded many in America and Ireland to renounce drink in the previous generation.

---

[66] 'Funeral of the Late Mr John Hulley', *Liverpool Mercury*, 12th January 1875.

[67] Hugh Stowell Brown, ed W S Caine, *Extracts from His Commonplace Book*, in *Hugh Stowell Brown, A Memorial Volume*, p 160.

[68] John Furnival, *Children of the Second Spring* (Leominster: Gracewing, 2005), p 201.

Father Matthew had visited Liverpool in 1843 and his influence in the cause of abstinence from alcohol was still present in the town when the baton was taken up by Father Nugent.

Nugent's influence for the cause of total abstinence was immense but was still mainly among Roman Catholics, and although Nugent and Brown had great admiration for one another their different religious traditions kept them from joining forces entirely. They certainly worked side by side in various causes and committees, and when Brown died Nugent attended Brown's funeral and praised his work most highly.

Part of Brown's temperance work was through the United Kingdom Alliance, of which he was a member and a regular speaker. The Alliance was founded in Manchester in 1853 as a political movement with the aim of prohibition: banning the sale of all alcohol in the United Kingdom. They did not see themselves as another Temperance Movement, but as a political campaign to remove the temptation of alcohol by preventing it from being sold.

It is unclear whether Brown wholeheartedly supported the Alliance in its prohibitionist policy, and this particular cause was taken up by his son-in-law William Caine. Caine developed his views on abstinence from the ministry of Brown, and with his wife Alice took them into the arena of national politics. Caine became vice-president of the United Kingdom Alliance. Caine was also president of the Baptist Total Abstinence Society, the Congregational Temperance Society, the British Temperance League and the National Temperance Federation. Caine served four terms as an MP from 1880 until his death in 1903, and although he rose to become Civil Lord of the Admiralty in Gladstone's government he was always held back from his potential as a politician by the position he maintained on temperance.

Hugh Stowell Brown's contribution to his adopted home of Liverpool was immense, in the people whose lives he influenced, in the progress of the churches he supported, and in the public service he gave to the town, and later city, of Liverpool. His work and his influence also reached out to the whole nation and to the generations that followed after him in a legacy that is measured more in people than in buildings or writings.

8

His American Adventure

On 15th August 1872 Hugh Stowell Brown set off on trip of a lifetime to see the up-and-coming nation of the United States. In leaving Liverpool bound for the New World, Brown was following in the wake of many emigrants and travellers who had used Liverpool as their port of embarkation. He described his eagerness to see America as 'one of the great desires of my life'.[69]

In the year 1872, forty-four steamships and sailing vessels belonging to the five major shipping lines made more than 300 crossings from Liverpool to New York. The Inman Line had eleven vessels and the Cunard Line had ten vessels regularly crossing the Atlantic. In all, over 167,000 passengers made the journey from Liverpool to New York in 1872 and en route seventy-nine people died and forty-five babies were born. The main cause of sickness and death on the voyage was smallpox, though no deaths were recorded in August 1872. Over half of all the passengers arriving in New York that year had begun their voyage in Liverpool.

---

[69] All comments by Hugh Stowell Brown in this chapter are taken from chapter 19, 'My Visit to America', in Hugh Stowell Brown, ed W S Caine, *Notes of My Life*, in *Hugh Stowell Brown, A Memorial Volume*, pp 100-121.

Links between Liverpool and the United States were not only in trade and commerce. Cultural links across the Atlantic included the regular visits of American preachers and religious missions to Liverpool. The first seven missionaries of the Mormons or Church of Jesus Christ of Latter-Day Saints to Britain had arrived in Liverpool in 1837. These were followed in 1840 by a second mission led by Brigham Young, and Liverpool became the headquarters and base for all Mormon activity in Britain for the rest of the century.

In 1841 the evangelist James Caughey had arrived from America and in 1842 received a call from God to lead a revival as he preached at Great Homer Street Chapel. The year after Hugh Stowell Brown's American trip, the American evangelist Dwight L Moody and his musician partner Ira B Sankey landed in Liverpool in June 1873 with the intention of 'winning 10,000 souls for Christ'. Their public meetings throughout Britain ended in a series of rallies in 1875 drawing crowds of up to 11,000 people to a temporary building erected on Victoria Street.

Arriving in New York

The ten-day voyage on a steamship in 1872 tested Brown's resilience against seasickness. He did manage to conduct a service on Sunday 18th August despite the rough conditions and the large rolling waves. Brown had come to America as a traveller and a tourist, but his reputation in New York was such that he had been booked to speak in two churches, four miles apart, on the afternoon and evening of the day his ship arrived in the city. This, he said, was the hottest day he had ever known, and even hotter in the churches, which were packed to overflowing with people eager to hear this Englishman.

It was only seven years since the end of the American Civil War and the United States was in a time of reconstruction. The Thirteenth Amendment abolished slavery in 1865 and the Fifteenth in 1870 had given the vote to all men regardless of race. This was the 'gilded age', a term coined by Mark Twain[70] to describe the era of American expansion, population growth and extravagant displays of wealth.

In his *Notes of My Life*, Brown records his trip to the United States as being in 1873, but his *Notes* and his memory are mistaken. He records how on his first day in New York he was plunged into the middle of the campaign for presidency of Horace Greeley. It was in 1872 that Greeley stood for the presidency, and in fact he died in November 1872 after the election but before the Electoral College ratified the result. Greeley was a New York newspaper editor who had himself visited Liverpool in 1851 en route to the Great Exhibition in London, and had not been impressed with the 'cold and stately' English. Had Greeley met Brown during his brief time in Liverpool he might have made a different judgement on the English as a race.

Greeley was the Liberal Republican candidate who carried the support of the Democratic Party, standing against the Republican incumbent Ulysses S Grant. The

---

[70] The phrase comes from the title of a novel: Mark Twain and Charles Dudley Warner, *The Gilded Age, A Tale of Today* (Hartford, CT: American Publishing Company, 1873).

Liberal Republican and Democratic Alliance was the nearest political grouping to the British Liberals, and like the Liberals in England had the support of the large majority of Baptists. Hugh recalls how the stifling heat of the church where he spoke caused all the ladies present to use fans to cool themselves, and most of the fans had a full-colour portrait of Horace Greeley on them. He records how 'a thousand portraits of Horace Greeley were waving up and down'. One such fan was presented to Hugh who used it to cool himself during the singing of the hymns.

In his two months in the United States and Canada, Hugh travelled over 5,400 miles. From the sprawling city of New York with a population three times the size of Liverpool, Hugh travelled by steamboat up the Hudson River to Albany, and then to Saratoga, of which he said, 'Saratoga is nowhere compared to our Leamington, or Cheltenham or Harrogate'.

O Canada and beyond

Hugh's journey then took him across the St Lawrence and the Canadian border to Montreal, which he called 'a very noble place'. From there he went by steamer to Ottawa and by rail back to the St Lawrence River, then another steamer took him through the 'Lake of One Thousand Islands' to Toronto, and then to Niagara. Like many tourists before and since, Hugh was enthralled by the Niagara Falls, declaring it to be 'worth a man's while to cross the Atlantic, if for no other purpose than that of seeing and hearing Niagara'.

Leaving behind the extraordinary sights of Niagara, Hugh crossed back into the United States and entered the great city of Chicago. In the previous year, 1871, Chicago had suffered a devastating fire which destroyed a third of the city, including most of the commercial area. Hugh reported that the city was rapidly rebuilding, and characteristically comments on the pay of the carpenters, sixteen shillings a day, and the apparent affluence of the working men.

After Chicago, Hugh relived his days as a railway worker on the long 1,400-mile journey west on the Union Pacific Railroad to Salt Lake City in Utah. Salt Lake City was and is the centre of the Mormon religion and Hugh's comments about Mormonism at Salt Lake City are indicative of his attitude to the sect. Evangelicals in the present day would consider Mormons to be a mistaken, maybe even dangerous, religion. Most would call Mormonism a cult and be very wary of its teachings and practice. It is revealing then that Hugh says, 'I spent a Sunday in Salt Lake City, and of course went to the Tabernacle.' He reports that the Tabernacle, the international headquarters building of the Mormon faith, was a grand building, able to hold 10,000 people, but on the day he attended only 1,000 were present. He says the service was 'the dullest I ever attended' and he had nothing better to say about the sermon, which Hugh considered to be 'neither law nor Gospel, but a virulent attack on the United States Government'.

Hugh then records an afternoon service, a communion service using water instead of wine, which was attended by Brigham Young, the worldwide leader of Mormons since the death of Joseph Smith in 1844 and the founder of Salt Lake City. By 1872 Young was an old man. Hugh records that he was there with 'several of his wives' and refers to him as 'the great prophet'. Hugh also noted that most of the Mormons he met in Salt Lake City were English, not Americans. On the Sunday evening Hugh preached at a small Baptist church in the city where he met a man from Liverpool who had attended Myrtle Street chapel many times. This man then introduced Hugh to his three wives. The practice of polygamy seems to have disturbed Hugh much more than the religious doctrines of the Salt Lake City Mormons, and he records that he was glad to get away from the 'disgusting place'.

Back to New York

Next stop was Denver, 500 miles east from Salt Lake City, and then just a small desert outpost. As the railway had only reached Denver in 1870, Hugh was one of the city's first international visitors and his stay was announced in the local newspaper. Then he travelled another 800 miles east to St Louis where the Mississippi River was crowded with huge steamboats. Hugh's next visit was to the Mammoth Cave in Kentucky, the longest cave system in the world and an international sensation in the nineteenth century, which impressed Hugh greatly.

From Kentucky another 600 miles east took him to Richmond, Virginia. He found the city 'besieged, battered and impoverished' after the Civil War. Richmond had been the capital of the Confederacy and the place where the war had ended when Robert E Lee's army had surrendered to

Ulysses S Grant and the Union army in 1865. A third of the city had been destroyed by fire and when Hugh Stowell Brown was there it was in the early days of reconstruction. In Richmond Hugh attended what he calls a 'coloured' church, attended by black former slaves. He describes the jubilation of people who had recently gained their freedom, although he records that the former slaves he spoke to all told him that they had been treated well. Hugh writes of the singing in that church: 'one man sings or intones a verse and the whole congregation joins in the chorus'.

From Richmond Hugh headed north on the last stage of his journey back towards New York. At Washington DC he took in the sights including the White House, then he visited Philadelphia and then Boston, which he considered a town full of self-importance. Hugh's experience of Boston was marred by the number of advertisements for spiritualists and mediums, which appalled him. The final destination of his journey was a visit to a friend in Connecticut before going back to New York for the ten-day voyage home.

Reflections from the New World

Three themes arise from Brown's journey of a lifetime to the United States and Canada. The first is his reflection on church life in America as compared to England. Hugh was at his core a voluntarist – he believed that commitment to Christ and to His Church had to be the choice of the individual without coercion or hindrance of any kind from the State. The existence of different denominations was a sign of a healthy society which allowed all viewpoints to flourish. America had a religious pluralism which Hugh had not seen in England, Scotland or any country in Europe. That was why he did not condemn the Mormons, although he did show an open criticism of spiritualists.

Hugh records the various expressions of faith in the United States as a testimony to 'the power of voluntaryism'. This is evidenced for him in the grandeur of some of the church buildings, some costing as much as £60,000 to build, and lavishly furnished. Hugh's interest in the price of everything leads him to comment on the payment of pew rents and the amount paid to the professional choir members. He comments on the amount the ministers are paid, more generously than in England, and how easy their life is compared to most English Free Church ministers.

One consequence of this lavish spending in the churches, in Hugh's consideration, was the lack of provision of churches for the poorer districts and for places away from the centres of population. Hugh admits that this is a weakness of 'voluntaryism' and is seen in Britain, but in America Hugh witnessed a particular neglect of poorer people, who could not pay the pew rents. His reflection was that in the United States, where religion was entirely left to the voluntary association of people and their voluntary donations, 'the tone of religious life and the character of religious ordinances are no higher than in our own country.'

The second lesson Hugh learned in the United States and Canada was about another of his lifelong concerns: drunkenness and temperance. As well as praising the

Mormons for their sobriety, Hugh remarked on the greater self-control of most of the people he met. On a steamer on the Ottawa River, for instance, he travelled with forty backwoodsmen who had access to the on-board bar and drank nothing stronger than tea all day. Hugh claims that he saw many working men on his trip but only ever saw two of them in a state of drunkenness. His conclusion was that 'America beats us in the matter of sobriety', but he does not reflect in his travel journal why this might be the case.

The third matter that Hugh draws attention to in America is that it was a nation of enterprise. Hugh was clearly impressed at the opportunities offered to all people from freed slaves to businessmen, and the way that the nation was rebuilding after the Civil War. He describes it as a 'country full of life, intelligence, enterprise', and one in which there is opportunity for every man who is willing to work. This work ethic was one that Hugh had often spoken about in his 'Lectures to Working Men', and it fitted well with his beliefs on social mobility and opportunities for people from a poorer background.

Brown clearly greatly enjoyed his visit to America. He ends his account by recommending such a trip to all his readers. He delights in the ease of communication with people who speak English, in the general cleanliness of the place and in the ease of travel.

His view of the United States was prescient. A country not many years out of civil war and still finding its feet as an independent nation would not inevitably become an international superpower. But Hugh finishes his account of his trip with this prophetic statement:

Undoubtedly a great and glorious future awaits it; its soil, its climate, its mineral treasures, its capacious harbours, its great lakes which are inland seas, its rivers, navigable for thousands of miles, its civil and religious liberty, its freedom from the hundred complications of European politics, its ability to live in peace and safety without the costly burdens of armaments such as those of France, Germany and Russia; all things seem to point a future of greatness that has never been equalled in the history of the world.[71]

[71] Hugh Stowell Brown, ed W S Caine, *Notes of My Life*, in *Hugh Stowell Brown, A Memorial Volume*, p 121.

9
National Recognition

When Hugh Stowell Brown was welcomed as the president of the Baptist Union for the year 1878–79 it was to general acclaim. The Baptist Union had been founded in 1813 as an organisation of the Particular Baptists, but it was restructured in 1833 to allow for membership of General Baptists. It was not until 1891 that General and Particular Baptists came together to form what we would recognise as the Baptist Union as it became in the twentieth century.

Presidential address

The Annual Session of the Baptist Union was held in London and began on Monday 29th April 1878 with the presidential address from 'Rev H. S. Brown of Liverpool'. He began his address by warning the gathered congregation that his subject 'will not be very deeply interesting'. He had chosen to speak on 'Ministerial Apprenticeship',[72] a paper that was a response to a discussion within the Congregational Union on 'Annual Curacies'.

---

[72] Hugh Stowell Brown, *Ministerial Apprenticeship, Address to the Annual Session of the Baptist Union, April 29th 1878* (London: Yates and Alexander, 1878).

Both this address and his second presidential address at the autumn session of the Baptist Union on Wednesday 9th October were rather dry and technical. This was not Brown the orator, who could delight large crowds with topical references, managing to connect the life of the common man to the erudite scholars of antiquity. These talks were Brown the church strategist. By now he was building a legacy based on thirty years' pastorate at Myrtle Street, many years of travelling among the Baptist churches and other churches of the British Isles, and some experience of the United States of America as well. These two addresses are the voice of experience.

In the April address he urges the larger Baptist churches to consider taking on young men (and all ministers were men at that time), people who had completed training at a Baptist college but who were not yet ready to take pastoral charge of a church. These he called 'ministerial apprentices'. He chooses not to use the word 'curate', the word that had been used in the Congregational Church discussion, and a word borrowed from the Anglican Church, but a word borrowed from industry, a work that spoke of ministry as a trade to be learned and honed. Hugh had himself served two apprenticeships – as a surveyor and as an engineer – before entering a formal theological education.

Hugh argued that in the New Testament the model of ministerial training, or 'ministerial formation' as it would be called today, was that of apprenticeship: Apollos learning from Aquila and Priscilla, John Mark learning from Paul and Barnabas. In this passage he is drawing his examples from the book of Acts chapters 12 to 18. In Baptist churches, he contended, unlike other churches, new ministers go straight from college into pastorate and, he said, 'this would be folly in business or in driving trains', and so it is in churches.

His presidential urging to the Baptist leaders gathered together was for larger churches, and groups of smaller churches, to take on newly trained ministers and allow them to learn from others. He also suggested that some senior ministers, some 'of our honoured brethren' as he called them, could be set free from the demands of pastoring one church to have the 'kindly oversight' of many churches. These would have to be men whose 'high character and long service have won the esteem of the whole denomination', who would encourage other ministers and help weaker churches.

This was an idea ahead of its time and has been adopted by British Baptist churches in the current system of Regional Ministry which works, when it works well, to, as Brown put it, 'put heart into many a despairing brother'. Brown was quick to defend his idea against claims that it was too much like bishops overseeing a diocese: 'We are not Prelatists,' he said, 'but we are Episcopalians.' As a theology exam paper would say: discuss.

The Union president gave a second address at the autumn assembly and in October his subject was even drier than his first, and it is difficult to see its purpose. Its title was: 'An Appeal to Young Men to Devote Themselves to the Work of the Christian Ministry'.[73] The title seems

---

[73] Hugh Stowell Brown, *An Appeal to Young Men to Devote Themselves to the Work of the Christian Ministry, An Address Delivered to the Autumnal*

straightforward enough – more young people were needed to serve as ministers in the Baptist Union then as they are now. But his address had one particular target in mind, and this is elucidated in the subtitle: 'An appeal to the well-educated and well-circumstanced young men of our denomination to devote themselves to the work of the Christian ministry'.

The lengthy address had one purpose – to persuade those young men who were from wealthy middle-class backgrounds, who had received the advantages of a good education, to go into Baptist ministry. Brown noted that many men going into the Baptist colleges were poor and illiterate. And while these people were not to be criticised, the denomination needed people of education and standing in society, so that the ministry could 'command very great respect'. Many a one of our students leaves college, he said, 'in mental culture inferior to many of the congregation which he is to instruct and whose respect he is to gain'.

Brown does note that some great men from the nonconformist tradition came from lowly background, people such as John Bunyan and William Carey, but he seemed sure that for the denomination to thrive it needed to attract more people from the 'better off classes'. As so often, money was part of the reason for his concern. Ministers with their own financial independence would not have to be a burden on small churches.

The address ends with the conclusion that 'in the ministry of the church, it is well that rich and poor should

Session of the Baptist Union, Wednesday October 9th 1878 (London: Yates and Alexander, 1878).

meet together. It ought not to be composed exclusively of either class.' Even with its conclusion, his choice of topic is a very strange one for a man who had been working for thirty years among the poor of Liverpool, as well as the rich, a man who had given much of his life to speaking in a plain and simple manner to the 'working man'. It can only be concluded that this was a topic that was needed for its time and place among this particular group of people.

It was just as he began his year as Baptist Union president that Brown acted on his own advice and took on an apprentice at Myrtle Street chapel, Rev Henry Lapham. But Lapham's role was nothing like the one Brown had outlined in his presidential address and, as has been described, Lapham's time at Myrtle Street did not go well. The tasks given to Henry Lapham were not all in keeping with Brown's plan for 'apprenticeship' outlined to the Baptist Union, and having an assistant at Myrtle Street did not suit Brown at all.

His friend Mr Spurgeon

Hugh Stowell Brown's national reputation can perhaps be demonstrated through his relationship with the Baptist preacher Charles Haddon Spurgeon. Spurgeon (1834–92) was called 'the Prince of Preachers' and is better remembered by history than Brown, partly because his work was done in London. Spurgeon was eleven years younger than Brown and Spurgeon looked up to Brown as a senior friend and colleague. It is clear from their correspondence that Spurgeon valued Brown's advice and the many helpful conversations they shared. According to

H. Stowell Brown

Hugh Stowell Brown portrait and autograph, 1879 (photo: public domain)

one biographer, W Y Fullerton, Spurgeon once said of Brown: 'There was room enough in his heart for all the fleets of Europe to anchor.'[74]

Spurgeon, like Brown, came from an Anglican family, and he joined the Particular Baptists after a conversion experience. He was only nineteen when he was called to be minister at New Park Street Chapel in Southwark in 1854. He was quickly recognised as an exceptional preacher and

[74] W Y Fullerton, *Charles Haddon Spurgeon: A Biography* (London: Williams and Norgate, 1920), chapter 9.

New Park Street Chapel, already the largest Baptist congregation in London, soon outgrew its building.

In 1861, Spurgeon's congregation moved to the newly constructed Metropolitan Tabernacle in the Elephant and Castle district of London. This was a brand-new purpose-built chapel, with seating for 5,000 and standing room for another 1,000 – the largest nonconformist church building of its day. The Tabernacle opened at the end of March 1861 and in the week of celebrations after its opening there was to be a service of believers' baptism, the first in the new baptistery. The preacher at this service on Tuesday 9th April was Hugh Stowell Brown, invited as a personal friend of C H Spurgeon, as a renowned preacher and defender of the cause of the Baptist position on baptism. Brown's text was Colossians 2:12, 'Buried with him in baptism, wherein also [you] are risen with him through the faith of the operation of God, who [has] raised him from the dead' (AV).

Writing a personal life of C H Spurgeon in 1892, his friend Robert Shindler remembered the celebrations of that remarkable week in 1861. He recalled how there was 'a sermon now and then on special subjects, notably one by Rev Hugh Stowell Brown of Liverpool on "Christian Baptism"'.[75]

An article in *The British Standard* magazine of 12th April 1861 reported on the events of that week:

---

[75] Robert Shindler, *From the Usher's Desk to the Tabernacle Pulpit: The Life and Labours of Charles Haddon Spurgeon* (London: Passmore and Alabaster, 1897), p 127.

On the evening of Tuesday, the ordinance of baptism by immersion was administered to some twenty people. It was eminently fitted to produce very serious consequences in families and churches. First came a sermon from a man of great mental power and pulpit efficiency, – Mr H.S. Brown, of Liverpool. The argument and the appeal being over, then followed the illustration by the skillful hand of Mr. Spurgeon.[76]

It might be claimed that 1861 was Hugh Stowell Brown's happiest year. He had been pastor at Myrtle Street for fourteen years: the building had been extended and its growth was still evident. There were plans for the planting of new churches in Liverpool and neighbouring towns. It was the year in which he preached to the largest congregation of his life, at the first baptism service at the largest Baptist church in the country, and he was acclaimed nationally for his gifts. It was the year in which the Lord Nelson Street lectures were coming to their natural end: lectures in which he had broken new ground, and lectures which were selling in their thousands in printed form. The Workman's Bank has been started and real plans were in place to alleviate poverty in Liverpool. And Hugh was living with his wife Alice, five children and three servants in Lime Street in Liverpool. It was the best of times.

---

[76] *The British Standard*, 12th April 1861.

Giving to the orphanage

Another major work for which Spurgeon is remembered, and in which Hugh Stowell Brown was involved, was the building of an orphanage in Stockwell in London, following the example of George Müller in Bristol. Brown was a supporter of the Stockwell Orphanage from the beginning and persuaded Myrtle Street Church to give generously to the work. The first phase of building was completed in 1869 and Shindler reported:

> Rev Hugh Stowell Brown of Liverpool and Rev J P Chown, then of Bradford, with their liberal-hearted people, raised large sums for the orphanage. Mr Brown's people sent £450 for the project.[77]

The completed orphanage only accommodated boys and there was a need for a section for girls and improved facilities, so fundraising activities continued. In 1880 the autumnal session of the Baptist Union was held in London, and the first meeting of the session was in Stockwell to visit the beginning of the building of the new phase of Spurgeon's orphanage. A south-west block was being added to the orphanage specifically for girls, designed by Alfred Wright. It was a terrace of six houses with schoolrooms above them, including a girls' play room and a swimming pool. One of the new houses in the purpose-built complex was to be called 'the Liverpool House' and was 'named in remembrance of the help given to the orphanage by friends in Liverpool'. The friends in Liverpool were the congregation of Myrtle Street Baptist

---

[77] Shindler, *From the Usher's Desk to the Tabernacle Pulpit*, p 172.

chapel, who had raised money for Spurgeon through the efforts of Brown, at the same time that he was working through the possibility of his resignation from the church. The 'memorial stone' of the Liverpool House was laid by Hugh Stowell Brown on Monday 4th October 1880.

One more series of correspondence serves to illustrate the relationship between Spurgeon and Brown and the respect in which they were both held within the Baptist community. Spurgeon was very often asked to speak at the Union's autumn session, but Hugh Stowell Brown was often the next in line to be the speaker should Spurgeon decline the offer. In 1881 the secretary of the Baptist Union was William Sampson, and he wrote to Spurgeon from 19 Castle Street, Holborn:

> When we feared, last autumn, that you might not be able to be with us, I wrote to Stowell Brown, asking him if he would be prepared to speak – and willing to speak or be silent, as you were able or not. By return of post came back the kindest letter consenting most gladly.[78]

In the end Spurgeon did preach at the autumnal session in Portsmouth and Southampton that October. The next year the autumnal session was held in Liverpool. Brown himself wrote to Spurgeon in June 1882 asking him to come to Liverpool in October to speak at the sessions 'in the name of the churches here'. Spurgeon replied, saying he

---

[78] Letter of 24th May 1881, quoted in C H Spurgeon, *Spurgeon's Autobiography Complied from His Diary, Letters and Records*, Vol 4, (London: Passmore and Alabaster, 1897), ch 93, p 150.

should not always be the preacher these special occasions. Brown replied, imploring Spurgeon to attend:

My Dear Mr Spurgeon,

We are all as desirous as ever that you should preach at the autumn meeting. I fully appreciate your hesitancy to take so prominent a place, and to do so arduous a work, year after year; but no one else can do it, and upon your advent so very much depends. I hope that, should you come, we can make a handsome collection for your Orphanage. I say this not as a bribe, – for your resources are in better hands than ours, and the Lord will not suffer them to fail; – but I say it as expressive of the love in which we hold you, and of our wish to do what we think would be gratifying to you.

I must now leave the decision to your own judgement, earnest hoping that you will come, yet very unwilling to impose upon you a work which, for various reasons, must be a heavy addition to your other burdens.

Yours faithfully

H Stowell Brown[79]

Brown and the Liverpool Baptists were clearly very keen to have Spurgeon as the speaker as they hosted the national meetings. Brown personally, along with the people of Myrtle Street, had given a lot of money and concern to Spurgeon's work in Stockwell, and for him to refuse to attend would have been a disappointment to them. For Hugh to entice Spurgeon with the 'carrot' of

---

[79] Quoted in ibid, p 151.

more funds for the orphanage and then to backtrack and say 'I say this not as a bribe' is so in keeping with his concern about money and his awareness of the persuasive power of money.

In the event, Spurgeon did travel to Liverpool and speak at the autumn session, held in St George's Hall and Myrtle Street chapel. The church minutes record:

> The Baptist Union of Great Britain and Ireland was welcomed to Liverpool with a service held at St George's Hall. The large hall was crowded. The meetings were continued in the Chapel on Tues 3rd, Weds 4th and on the evening of Thurs 5th were brought to a close by a united communion service held in the chapel. The chapel was filled by ministers, delegates and the members of various Baptist churches in the town.[80]

The offering for the orphanage raised the large sum of £131 5s 6d. The address in Liverpool was to be Spurgeon's last-ever address to the Baptist Union, and as far as we know the last meeting of these two great Baptists of the nineteenth century.

---

[80] Minute-Book of Myrtle Street Baptist Church, Liverpool, October 1882.

10
His Home Life

Hugh Stowell Brown writes very little about his domestic life in his memoirs, *Notes of My Life*, and there is not much in the published version of his *Commonplace Book* to help us uncover much of a personal nature. What we know of Hugh's home life has to be pieced together from contemporary accounts and census records.

We do know that Hugh grew up in a large family. His childhood and youth in a small parsonage in Douglas then in Kirk Braddan were experiences shared by many of his time. Hugh was one of ten children of whom two, as we have seen, died in childhood: John, aged two and Harry, aged fourteen. The family had it much better than most, growing up in reasonable affluence and in the countryside.

Hugh himself was a healthy man, even into his later years. He often gave thanks in his *Commonplace Book* for his good health. In January 1865 he recorded that he had 'not had one day's illness'.[81] Other than one serious illness in 1876, he remained healthy until the day of his death. It was reported that he was full of energy to his very last day and could have walked twenty miles without getting tired just

---

[81] Hugh Stowell Brown, ed W S Caine, *Extracts from His Commonplace Book*, in *Hugh Stowell Brown, A Memorial Volume*, p 140.

the week before he died. But he knew the pain of suffering and loss and nursed both his wives up to their death.

Alice, the mother of his children

Hugh's first wife was Alice Chibnall Sirrett. He and Alice met at Stony Stratford Baptist Church. Alice's father was John Sirrett of Stony Stratford and her mother was Catherine Chibnall whose family were from Passenham, a tiny village a mile outside Stony Stratford.

Hugh and Alice were married by Mr Forster at Stony Stratford Baptist Church on Tuesday 9th May 1848, six months after Hugh has been taken on as the permanent minister at Myrtle Street. Hugh was twenty-four and his wife a year older.

The couple lived at 9 South Myrtle Street, just next to Myrtle Street chapel. Their first child was a girl, called Alice after her mother, and the second followed soon after, born in April 1850 and named Robert after his uncle and paternal grandfather, both of whom had died less than four years before. In the census of March 1851 the Browns are a family of four living with two servants: Elizabeth Pearce, aged twenty-five, from Abergele, in North Wales, and Jane Crow, aged seventeen, from the Isle of Man. With so many needy people in Liverpool it seems strange that neither of the two servants were from the town, though they may have been daughters of families who had moved there.

Hugh was probably not the most attentive of fathers. His early attempts at running a Sunday school convinced him that he was not a natural with children. We know he worked very long hours and it is likely that he had little to do with his own children when they were young. He was, however, moved to great grief when on 26th August 1851 young Robert died, aged just sixteen months, the third generation of 'Robert Browns' to die within five years. Later that same year their third child was born and was given his father's full name, Hugh Stowell Brown.

Two years later Alice gave birth to the couple's fourth child and third son, and he was given another family name, John Sirrett Brown after his maternal grandfather, who had died when Alice was a young girl. Then on 15th November 1854 Hugh Stowell Brown junior died, aged three. The death of any child is heartbreaking, even in times when so many children died young, but the death of Hugh's oldest living son, who had been given his own name, must have been especially hard to bear. A generation later it was left to John to pass on the name Hugh Stowell Brown to his first son, born in 1879, and that Hugh also called his first son Hugh Stowell Brown, born in 1913.

A few weeks later another daughter was born, named Dora after Hugh's younger sister who died on the Isle of Man the following year, aged twenty-seven. By this time the couple had three children: Alice was six and John was two when Dora was born. There were then no more children for three years, the longest gap Alice had between children. In 1858 another daughter was born and named Bertha after Hugh's Aunt Bertha, his mother's sister. Then in 1859 another girl came along, named Eleanor. The family now had five children under ten and was getting to be handful for Alice, even though she had servants to help her.

In the 1861 census the family are living at 97 Lime Street, which was a larger house than the one in South Myrtle Street. As well as Hugh, Alice and the five children, there are three other people listed in the house, described as 'house servants'. The three maids were Rachel Collan, aged twenty-three, and Harriet Harwell, aged sixteen, both from Liverpool, and Mary Pike, aged twenty-five, from Ireland. In February 1862 Alice gave birth to the couple's eighth and last child, a boy named Frederick Thomson Brown. Again there was a family connection in the name: Thomson was the maiden name of Hugh's mother, Dorothy.

Losing his beloved

One of the three great tragedies of Hugh's life was the death of his wife Alice. Although two of their children had died very young, it was the death of Alice which affected him most, ranking alongside the death of his father. Alice was forty-one years old when she died on 24th August 1863. She and Hugh had been married for fifteen years. At the beginning of 1865 Hugh wrote in his *Commonplace Book*, 'I have had trials, severe and awful, especially the irreparable loss of my dear wife Alice in August 1863.'[82] He goes on to say that the experience of Alice's death had made him a stronger man in self-knowledge and more able to sympathise with others who had known loss. He says of the experience of Alice's death, 'I think that I can say that these afflictions have been of inestimable service'.[83]

---

[82] Ibid.
[83] Ibid.

One of Hugh's closest friends in Liverpool was Charles Birrell, a Scotsman who was minister of Pembroke Chapel, one of the largest nonconformist chapels in the town. Birrell was a dozen years older than Hugh and was a friend and mentor for many years. In 1871 Birrell was the president of the Baptist Union, seven years before Hugh received that honour. In character Birrell was quite the opposite of Hugh Stowell Brown, and was described by a contemporary as 'formal, courteous, refined and humourless'. But Birrell's ministry was a very similar one to Hugh's, promoting good causes among the poor of the town. Birrell's wife, Harriet, was well respected for her good works and was the first cousin of the social reformer Josephine Butler. Birrell had conducted the funeral service for Alice Brown, and then Harriet Birrell died suddenly in December 1863, just four months after the death of Alice.

Hugh delivered the memorial sermon after Harriet's death, based on Paul's words in 2 Corinthians 4:17, 'our light affliction, which is but for a moment, worketh for us a far more exceeding and eternal weight of glory' (AV).[84] In his sermon he explains the meaning of the text in the light of our 'afflictions', including the 'sorrows' of life. Speaking about the death of the wife of a close friend so soon after the death of his own wife, we are justified in seeing in the text Hugh's reflection on his own grief, even though he does not mention his own recent bereavement explicitly.

---

[84] 'The Effect of Sanctified Affliction', in Hugh Stowell Brown, ed W S Caine, *Extracts from His Commonplace Book*, in *Hugh Stowell Brown, A Memorial Volume*, pp 497-508.

Hugh has three points in his sermon in memory of Harriet Birrell. The first point is that Paul calls our afflictions 'light'. He says that our afflictions are light because they are light compared to what Paul suffered, to what we deserve to suffer, and to what Jesus suffered. He reflects on the vulnerability of human life and the way in which the more joys we have, the more we are vulnerable to afflictions. His second point is that the way we deal with afflictions depends on our attitude to eternity. Many people, he says, are brought down by grief and suffering, driven to drink, to despair or to suicide. But when we have the perspective of eternity then we see the eternal realities of life and death. When we fix our eyes on 'things that are not seen' (see 2 Corinthians 4:18), then we are not dragged down by life's circumstances. Thirdly, he says if we have the right perspective then our 'afflictions' work out for us an eternal glory. The greatest of these glories, according to Hugh, is not the glory of 'a title to enter heaven' but the glory on earth of the 'sanctified character'. Suffering makes us stronger and better people. He says that the person who, despite his afflictions, can say with Job, 'the Lord gave, and the Lord hath taken away; blessed be the name of the Lord', is 'a more gentle man, a more loving and tender-hearted man, a more heavenly-minded man than he was before'. He continues in poetic vein:

> In the silence of his sorrow he has heard that still small voice that is too still and small to be heard amidst the noise and bustle of ordinary life; in the wilderness of woe God speaks to him more comfortably than he ever did in the fields of prosperity and the gardens of joy; in the dark night

of his adversity a thousand stars of promise, that could not be seen in the glare of worldly happiness, have been beheld by him and have shed their consolatory influence upon his heart; the man's character has been wondrously improved, provided always that he had faithfully looked to the things that are not seen.[85]

When he speaks of 'the man's character' he is speaking to Charles Birrell in his loss and to all who have known suffering, but he is surely also speaking about himself and his own grief in the death of his beloved Alice. In that light these words are tender and moving.

Phoebe his helpmeet

So Hugh was left alone with six children, the eldest being fourteen and the youngest a baby of just eighteen months. It is in this loss that Hugh finds comfort from the Caine family. Nathaniel Caine was the man who had started the Concert Hall lectures back in 1854. Nathaniel's daughter Phoebe was then a single woman of twenty-five, and it would have been natural for her to offer her pastor some help with the children. Phoebe's mother had died some years previously and Phoebe had become the woman of the house, caring for her young sister and two brothers. Phoebe's help with the Browns led to affection between Hugh and Phoebe, and in June 1865, just short of two years after Alice's death, they were married.

---

[85] From 'The Effect of Sanctified Affliction', ibid, p 508.

Phoebe took on responsibility for the welfare of a man of some substance, known for his generous hospitality, and the care of his six children. It was a weighty undertaking, but it seems that Phoebe was up to the task and the household was described as 'serene and happy',[86] and the reputation for good hospitality continued as strongly as before.

Hugh writes of Phoebe with love and tenderness, calling her 'my darling' in his *Commonplace Book*, but Hugh and Phoebe had no children together. This may mean that they had a sexless marriage, or that there was some medical problem, or that they were careful to conceive no children: we don't know. We do know that they had nineteen years together in what seemed by all accounts to be a happy marriage. The pain of loss was not over for Hugh, however, and his youngest child, Frederick, died aged just four in December 1866.

Myrtle Street chapel, date unknown (photo: public domain)

---

[86] W S Caine, Preface, ibid, p vi.

Spreading their wings

Two years later the eldest daughter, Alice, who was by then aged nineteen, left home to marry William Sproston Caine. William Caine was Phoebe's brother, younger than her by three years, and at twenty-three was closer in age to Hugh's wife than to his daughter. Alice and William had met when William, along with two brothers, James and Samuel Smith, had started a Sunday service in the Union Rooms in Egremont, Wallasey, a meeting that became Serpentine Road Family Church. Nathaniel Caine and his family lived on Church Road in Egremont and, although the family's loyalty was to Myrtle Street, they wanted to promote a Baptist cause in their own community. William Caine wrote years later how that small meeting was the place he 'got a love for mission work'. Each week Caine would read a sermon by the London Baptist preacher Charles Haddon Spurgeon. While he was reading one of Spurgeon's sermons – number 391 – about those who are martyrs for Christ in Revelation chapter 20, a young girl barely in her teens made a public decision to follow Christ. She was Alice Brown, eldest daughter of the pastor of the mother church in Liverpool.

Alice and William's wedding ceremony was held in Myrtle Street chapel on 24th March 1868 and was conducted by Rev J P Chown, a Baptist minister and popular orator from Rochdale who went on to be president of the Baptist Union some years later. In marrying Alice, William Caine became both Hugh's son-in-law and his brother-in-law.

Caine grew up in the world of commerce and was a businessman through and through. For their honeymoon,

William took Alice on a tour of Wales for six weeks in a dog cart, calling on the customers of the family firm as they went. Wherever they stayed they told the hoteliers they were on their honeymoon and gained free accommodation in every hotel. The couple set up home at River View in Seacombe and crossed the river by the steamboat ferry twice each Sunday to attend worship at Myrtle Street.

In 1871 they moved to Princes Park in Liverpool, where Alice nearly died from a prolonged fever. Hugh wrote in his *Commonplace Book* of his concern for his daughter, 'My daughter Alice desperately ill, her husband and I looking almost hourly for her death these three weeks.'[87] He tells of how fervently he prayed, 'There is so much prayer for her. I never knew so well the meaning of "pray without ceasing" and yet I do not pray for her recovery in an unconditional manner. I pray that I might believe that what God does to be right.'[88] Alice remained unwell for a long time and the family moved to New Brighton in 1874 for Alice's health, then back to Liverpool two years later when they moved into prestigious accommodation in Rodney Street. The couple had five children: three girls who married doctors or MPs, and two boys who became a barrister and a doctor. Their daughter Hannah married John Roberts, the Welsh Liberal politician, in 1893. Roberts was elected an MP in 1892, made a baronet in 1902 and Baron Clwyd in 1919. Hannah thus became the first Baroness Clwyd and the great-grandmother of the current 4th Baron Clwyd, John Murray Roberts. It is interesting to speculate what Hugh Stowell Brown would think of his

---

[87] Ibid, p 139.
[88] Ibid.

great-grandson and his descendants having a hereditary peerage.

As previously mentioned, William was committed all his life to the Temperance Movement. He and Alice led the Egremont Band of Hope, with William leading the meetings and Alice playing the harmonium for the hymns. The couple joined the Liverpool Temperance and Band of Hope Union, and William served as chairman of the Popular Control and Licensing Reform Association. Alice supported William in his work for the United Kingdom Alliance, and the other temperance groups in which he served.

William was a high-achieving businessman and politician. By 1864 he was a partner in his father's iron merchant firm and travelled extensively in the United States and Canada. By 1878, at the age of forty-six, William retired from business to devote his time to 'public life'. In 1880 he was elected Liberal MP for Scarborough and was soon after appointed to a ministry post in the Admiralty by Liverpool-born Prime Minister, William Gladstone. In 1886 he was elected MP for Barrow-in-Furness, where his father's firm had owned most of the iron industry. He left the Liberals to join a breakaway party called the Liberal Unionists, and became their chief whip, but had to resign the post because his temperance stance damaged the party's alliance with the Conservatives. Caine might have achieved more in politics if he had taken a more conciliatory stance on temperance, but he was a principled politician and the senior Baptist in parliament right through to the dawn of the twentieth century.

By the census of 1871 Hugh was forty-seven and he and Phoebe were living at 26 Falkner Street with three children, one boarder and three servants. The house is in a desirable, four-storey eighteenth-century terrace, very close to Myrtle Street chapel. John was still living at home, aged seventeen. Bertha was thirteen and Eleanor was twelve. Dora, who was sixteen, was not living with her parents. The boarder living in the house is a sixteen-year-old boy listed as 'W. W. Brown' of Ash near Whitchurch in Shropshire, which was also the home village of Mary Emily Neild who was living in Liscard in Wirral in 1871 and who married John in 1878.

Weddings and blessings

Hugh Stowell Brown's household with Alice and with Phoebe was known for generous and lively hospitality. Their home in Falkner Street was convivial, with time always available for visitors. Sunday teatime was a particular occasion when many people from the church and wider community would be at the manse, sharing food and conversation with the Browns, though Hugh would most often retire to his study to complete his evening sermon during the afternoon.

The next few years were the time for weddings in the Brown family. John married Mary Neild in 1878. On 19th September the same year his sister Dora married Rev David Alexander Taylor DD, a Northern Irish Presbyterian minister, who had been ordained and inducted as minister of Second Comber Presbyterian Church in Comber, County Down, the previous year.

Their second son was named Hugh Stowell Brown Taylor and became a barrister of the Irish courts in Dublin in 1908. Another son, Alfred Squire Taylor, born in Belfast in 1889, was educated at Edinburgh university where he was president of the University Union and captain of the University Rugby Union team, and represented Ireland at Rugby four times in 1910 and 1912. He was killed on the first day of the third Battle of Ypres, 31st July 1917.

In 1880 Bertha, then aged twenty-two, married Morton Haig. They went on to have five children, named Alice, Cecil, Winifred, Bertha and Jack. That left only young Eleanor unmarried, though by the census of 1881 she too had left home.

Hugh's eldest surviving son, John, went into the building trade. In the second half of the nineteenth century, Liverpool and Wirral were expanding rapidly. There was need for the rapid increase in new buildings. Affordable new homes were needed for families leaving the city slums, and landmark buildings were springing up across the city region. John formed a building company called Brown and Backhouse, based in Chatham Street, to provide employment for local labourers and to offer quality local craftsmanship for the new buildings in the city. Their heyday was the late 1880s when the firm was responsible for some significant Merseyside buildings. In 1889 to 1890 they built Holy Trinity Church in Formby for the architect C A Atkinson, and in 1889 to 1892 the firm built the Victoria Building for University College Liverpool, now the University of Liverpool, with the architect Alfred Waterhouse. The Victoria Building was the university's first purpose-built building and it became the university's headquarters. A Gothic design, built in red brick with a terracotta dressing, this building was the inspiration for the term 'red-brick university'. It is now used as the university's museum and is known as the Victoria Gallery and Museum.

John and Mary had two children, Hugh Stowell Brown and Beta Manning Brown. They lived in the same grand Georgian house at 274 Upper Parliament Street in the Toxteth Park area of Liverpool where John had previously lived with his parents, and just a short walk from where his parents now lived in Falkner Square. John lived until 1922, by which time his son Hugh had two children of his own, another Hugh Stowell Brown and another John Brown.

More sadness and loss

In the census of 1881, we find Hugh living at 29 Falkner Square. The house is an elegant Georgian terraced house facing an open-grassed square and is very much the same today as it was when the Browns lived there. It is no bigger than their previous house in Falkner Street, but still is plenty large enough for the household of six people. This comprised of Hugh and Phoebe and four servants. The four were Maria Prudence, aged twenty-nine, Mary Hutchinson, twenty-five, and Alice Pinder (transcribed in the census as Pinda), eighteen, all from Scawby in Lincolnshire and Hanna(h) J Edward, aged nineteen, from Broughton-in-Furness. The connection with Broughton is a simple one: that was the town where the Caine family ironworks was based, so presumably Hannah Edward had connections with the Brown family through William and Alice. But the connection with Scawby is less easy to trace.

In 1881 Scawby, near Scunthorpe, was a village of just over 1,000 people. There was no Baptist church there, although the neighbouring Scawby Brook had a mission hall. Nearby Brigg was a railway centre but there is no evidence that Hugh ever visited Scawby or anywhere near it. Both Pinder and Hutchinson remain as surnames in Scawby, but their connection with Hugh Stowell Brown is not known.

In 1881 Hugh was fifty-seven and Phoebe was forty-two, but it was the beginning of an untimely end for them both. Phoebe soon developed a painful illness which caused as much distress to Hugh as it did to his wife. For three years Hugh slowly watched his wife's health deteriorate, and his attentions to her did nothing to improve her condition. It would have reminded him of how he sat with his daughter Alice through a long illness from which she recovered, and reminded him even more of how his first wife, Alice, had died. Phoebe was diagnosed with 'consumption', the term used at the time for tuberculosis, an infectious lung disease, and she may also have had cancer of the lung. Hugh wrote in his *Commonplace Book* of his prayers for his wife. On Sunday 17th February 1884 he wrote:

> My dear Phoebe is so ill and weak that I have constant sorrow and pain in my heart, she gets feebler and feebler, happily not suffering very much, but she is less and less capable of being interested in anything. She is very unselfish and complaining; when a little brighter she is wonderfully hopeful, but

that is no good sign; consumption has made her its prey, and hope has all but left me. I find it very hard in these dreadfully depressing circumstances to do my work, yet work is the best thing for me. Lord, help me to say, 'Thy will be done;' but oh! that it may be Thy will to spare her![89]

There are just two more entries in the *Commonplace Book*, which was Hugh's sounding board and companion. The next one is five weeks later, on Tuesday 25th March:

It is not His will – my darling died this morning without a struggle. It is a fine day, befitting the event – the departure of one so bright and cheerful. It is a great blow to me and to us all, but we have had nearly nineteen years of happy wedded life, and for this it behoves me to be profoundly thankful to God. I now have another treasure in Heaven.[90]

The Myrtle Street minutes for that same day record:

This day died to the great grief of the church Mrs Brown, the wife of our pastor. She was the daughter of the late Nathaniel Caine, deacon of the church. Throughout her connection with the church she manifested the warmest interest in its affairs, and she was a generous supporter of any form of Christian usefulness. The poor had no better friend than she.[91]

---

[89] Ibid, Preface, p vi.
[90] Ibid, Preface, p vii.
[91] Minute-Book of Myrtle Street Baptist Church, Liverpool, entry for 25th March 1884.

Phoebe was buried at the Necropolis, Everton, on the Friday and on the Sunday Dr Alexander Maclaren came from Manchester to speak at Myrtle Street. Phoebe was forty-five, just four years older than Alice had been when she died. Hugh suffered the sadness, emptiness and helplessness of bereavement again. But now aged sixty himself and living alone, he was less able to take the loss. The next entry in his *Commonplace Book* was to be his last. He wrote it on 25th March 1885:

> I have not had the heart to enter anything since this day twelve months. Now the sad anniversary has come. The event has proved a great shock to me, and made me sad and low all the year through. But I have had and continue to have good health, and my work, pretty constantly engaged in, has saved me. I have much reason to thank God, and I hope to work on a while longer.[92]

That 'while longer' proved to be just eleven months. Hugh remained physically in good health, but overwork and the loss of Phoebe were too much for him, and on Saturday 20th February 1886 he was completing his Sunday morning sermon when he had a stroke, and he died peacefully at home on the morning of Wednesday 24th February and went to meet his Lord at the age of sixty-two.

---

[92] Hugh Stowell Brown, ed W S Caine, *Extracts from His Commonplace Book*, in *Hugh Stowell Brown, A Memorial Volume*, Preface, p vii.

11
His Death and His Legacy

Hugh Stowell Brown's death was a heavy blow to the people of Liverpool, to Baptists throughout the British Isles and most especially to the members of his church.

Brown's funeral was arranged quickly. He died on the Wednesday morning and the funeral was held on the Saturday following. It began with a service at Myrtle Street chapel at ten o'clock, led by three Liverpool Baptist ministers and attended by many more ministers and church leaders. The address was given by Rev Richard Richards, who had taken over from Brown's close friend Charles Birrell as minister at Pembroke Chapel. Richards, who would not have known Brown as well as most of the congregation knew him, delivered what to the modern reader seems to be a message of sentiment and pathos. He spoke of Brown's energy in his later years, his wise counsel and his kindly teaching.

The public funeral

At eleven o'clock that morning the public funeral began with a gathering at the family home at 29 Falkner Square, from where the funeral cortège began the mile-and-a-half procession to the burial ground in Everton. Hugh was laid to rest in the Everton Necropolis (Low Hill Cemetery), which was then the burial ground for nonconformists and was where his first wife, Alice, their three children Robert, Hugh and Frederick, and his second wife, Phoebe, were all buried. The wording on his granite headstone simply read:

In Loving Memory of
Hugh Stowell Brown,
Pastor of Myrtle Street Chapel for nearly XXXVIII years.
Who fell asleep FEBy XXIV. MDCCCLXXXVI.
Aged LXIII years

Both the death notice in the local newspaper and the headstone for his grave claimed that Brown was aged sixty-three at his death, but both are incorrect. He died six months before his sixty-third birthday. The headstone is now lost. The Necropolis closed for burials in 1898. There is now little evidence of the cemetery: the gravestones were removed in 1913 and the public green space that remains is known as Grant Gardens.

The procession to the Necropolis and the service there were a testimony to the affection that the people of Liverpool had for Hugh Stowell Brown, a man of the people. The *Liverpool Echo* gave a full page to its coverage of the funeral on the evening of the event. In its section on the service at the cemetery the paper reported:

Seldom, if ever, in the history of this city has a larger or more representative gathering been seen at the burial ground of the Baptists at the Necropolis, where the body of the deceased minister, who had made for himself so great a name amongst Nonconformists was to be interred. The hour fixed

191

for the funeral was twelve, noon, but for more than an hour before that time a stream of people, many of whom were attired in mourning, passed continuously along the roads leading to the Necropolis, and long before the time fixed for the interment the cemetery was surrounded by a crowd of mourners. If any proof were needed of the widespread influence of the late Rev. Hugh Stowell Brown, and the catholicity, breadth of his sympathies, and the ready and universal response with which they were met, it might have been found in the crowd of mourners there for they were of all creeds and shades of religion – Establishment, Catholicism and Nonconformity were all represented by their leading men. After some delay, during which the crowd largely increased, until it numbered some 6,000 or 7,000, the funeral cortège arrived.[93]

As well as the thousands of mourners who attended on foot, the procession consisted of eleven carriages and many significant figures from the religious and secular community of Liverpool, Lancashire and beyond. The procession was led by the Liverpool Manx Association, and representatives of the Liverpool Peace Society. Among the church leaders from beyond the nonconformist community was a leading Anglican Canon, Thomas Major Lester (1829–1903), vicar of St Mary's Kirkdale, who, like Brown, worked for the poor of the town. Also present was Monsignor James Nugent (1822–1905), mentioned earlier, a Roman Catholic priest who was a tireless advocate of the

---

[93] *Liverpool Echo*, 27th February 1886.

poor and child welfare, and campaigner for the Temperance Movement and abstinence from alcohol. Lester and Nugent both have statues in their memory in St John's Gardens in Liverpool.

The funeral service at the Necropolis was led not by a Baptist, but by Rev Edward Hassan of Wavertree Congregational Church, who had been the minister at that church and a colleague of Hugh Stowell Brown for twenty-four years. His words were in stark contrast to the words of Richards in Myrtle Street, words that Brown would be happier to have heard: he said that instead of a 'eulogy to their departed friend', the people gathered there should 'address themselves to almighty God'.

The coffin, the newspapers reported, was 'literally covered with a beautiful arrangement of lilies, white roses, camellias, hyacinths, ivy and evergreens'. After the funeral had ended the principal mourners left, but the public remained, and others arrived; thousands visited the grave, many with wreaths and flowers to show their gratitude and devotion to a man Liverpool loved and had now lost.

The Everton Necropolis, around 1912 (photo: public domain)

His church says farewell

The next day was Sunday and the day for the morning and evening congregations at Myrtle Street Church to consider the loss of their beloved pastor.

At short notice the preacher at Myrtle Street that morning was to be the only Baptist preacher in the north of England of comparable reputation to Brown: Dr Alexander Maclaren of Manchester. Maclaren, unlike Brown and Spurgeon, was born into a Baptist home. He was born and brought up in Glasgow and entered Stepney College in London at the age of sixteen. A gifted scholar, he won prizes in Hebrew and Greek at London university and became renowned as a preacher. He served as minister of Union Chapel, Oxford Road, Manchester from 1858 until 1905.

The fact that a man such as Maclaren was willing to give up his plans for that day and to travel from Manchester to Liverpool to be at Myrtle Street chapel that morning (there is no mention of his attendance at the funeral the previous day), is a witness to his respect for Brown and his concern for the people at Myrtle Street. According to the report in the *Liverpool Echo*, every seat was full that morning and the aisles were filled with people standing as Maclaren chose as his text, from the Revised Version, Hebrews 13:7-8: 'Remember them that had the rule over you, which spake unto you the word of God; and considering the issue of their life, imitate their faith. Jesus Christ is the same yesterday and [to-day], yea[,] and for ever.'

Maclaren spoke about Brown the preacher, Brown the pastor and Brown the man. As a preacher, he said, Brown worked hard and delivered simple and powerful messages: 'His style of speech was all his own, simple and direct, the very perfection of manly preaching, full of many a sparkle of humour, with many a proverb and epigram.' He spoke of Brown's appeal to 'the common people' and his 'bluntness of speech'. This did not, however, make him unkind in character. He spoke, Maclaren said:

> with all the certitude and conviction and enthusiasm for the right, which was the characteristic of the old Hebrew prophets. Such was Hugh Stowell Brown for forty years in the knowledge of all England. But they knew how much of gentleness was in him – a gentleness which looked out of the eyes so kindly as well as keenly, and which played in many a sweet and gracious word, or a smile about the mobile lips.[94]

That Sunday evening at Myrtle Street chapel the preacher was Rev Samuel Pearson, the minister at Great George Street Chapel, the chapel where Brown had worshipped and heard the great Thomas Raffles preach back in November 1846. Pearson had taken over as minister at Great George Street in 1869 and had worked alongside Brown for seventeen years.

Pearson spoke to the grief of the congregation. Rather that eulogising Brown, he spoke about God meeting His people in their tribulations and providing 'an unseen source of consolation'. He spoke simply of Hugh Stowell Brown saying that he might have made a 'wider name for himself' and a lot more money in another profession, but 'by no possibility could he have lived a more useful and

---

[94] *Liverpool Echo*, 1st March 1886.

ennobling life outside the ranks of the Christian ministry, and right nobly did he bend every energy to the fulfilment of God's plan concerning him'.

Tributes from other churches

According to the reports in the local press, nearly every church in Liverpool, Baptist and otherwise, made mention of the passing of Brown that Sunday. His death was marked with sadness and loss by the whole Christian community of the town and beyond. In Toxteth Tabernacle, the church's founding pastor William Lockhart spoke of the 'sudden departure of our much-esteemed brother, Hugh Stowell Brown', and mentioned his 'character, keenness of mental vision' and 'fidelity to His service'.

At his own church that morning, Samuel Pearson had taken as his text Matthew 24:46, based on the Revised Version, 'Blessed is that servant whom his master, when he comes, will find so doing', and spoke of Brown as 'an honoured and a diligent and faithful servant of Christ'. In the Raffles Memorial Chapel in Greenland Street, Rev G Harris took the text, 'Moses my servant is dead' (see Joshua 1:2, AV). In Mount Pleasant Presbyterian Church Rev John Mackenzie took his text from 2 Timothy 4:7-8: 'I have fought a good fight, I have finished my course, I have kept the faith' (AV), and spoke of the Christian, his conflict and his crown, all the time referring to the life of his friend Hugh Stowell Brown.

At Park Road Baptist Church in St Helens, a church planted by Myrtle Street under the leadership of Hugh

Stowell Brown in 1869, their founder was remembered and the pulpit there was draped in black cloth. Rev W C Tayler, who was minister at Park Road and at the Baptist Church at Earlestown, spoke at the latter of the bereavement felt by all Baptists and especially the members in Myrtle Street and its 'branch missions'.

One of the biggest nonconformist churches in Birkenhead, across the Mersey from Liverpool, was Grange Road Presbyterian Church, where the pastor was Rev William Hutton. Hutton was a Scot, born in 1834, and had come to Birkenhead in 1880, where he was known as a wise pastor and was recognised nationally as Moderator of the General Synod of the Presbyterian Church of England in 1898. Hutton spoke about his friend Hugh that Sunday morning at the end of his sermon on Shadrach, Meshach and Abednego, who were thrown into a fiery furnace for their faith (see Daniel 3). He said:

> I feel I cannot close without referring to the great loss that all the churches have sustained by the unexpected removal by the death of Hugh Stowell Brown of Liverpool. I have felt that it is most fitting to refer to him in connection with those three heroic Hebrews. There was much in him of the stuff of which martyrs are made. He was distinguished among his fellows by his courage, his independence, his unflinching adherence to what he believed to be the cause of righteousness; and as a valiant defender of the faith, and one to whom most of us could turn for sympathy and comfort. A very tower of strength he was in the interest of the Church. His voice had ever a truly manly ring in it, and it was the true

interpretation of an honest heart he preached. He had no tolerance for anything like affectation, or selfishness, or littleness; but he had a just liking for good men and true men to whatever class or school they belonged. He loved the society of his brethren and was repaid with much of their love and honour in return; and now he will be sincerely lamented and sadly missed now he is gone.[95]

It was not only Baptists and nonconformists who remembered his work. At St Mary's Church, Edge Hill, Rev John Turnbull spoke of 'the lamented death of the Rev Hugh Stowell Brown' and that 'this city had lost one of its most philanthropic and zealous citizens'. One High Church Anglican priest who was later sent to prison for his religious views spoke of his admiration for Brown. Rev James Bell Cox was Anglican vicar of St Margaret's Church in the Princes Park area of Liverpool and was for many years at the centre a controversy about his use of Catholic ritual. But on the Sunday after the death of Hugh Stowell Brown he spoke well of a man who was opposed to many of his beliefs. Bell Cox is reported to have said in his evening sermon: 'Since last Sunday a great gap has been created in our midst as citizens by the disappearance from among us a prominent and remarkable figure, who beyond question exercised a great power among the members of his own denomination and many outside it also.'[96]

The most remarkable tribute to Hugh Stowell Brown from outside Baptist circles was given by Monsignor James

---

[95] Ibid.
[96] Ibid.

Nugent – Father Nugent as he was known. On the evening of Brown's funeral Nugent was speaking at the People's Free Concert at the Rotunda Hall in William Brown Street and, according to the report in the *Liverpool Echo*, he said:

> It is only a few weeks ago – about a month, I think – since there was in that chair (indicating the chairman's seat on the platform) one whose loss Liverpool truly mourns this day. To measure Liverpool's affection and veneration for him, one only had to see the crowds of people that thronged within the walls of the Necropolis and mark their demeanour this morning when the funeral took place. A month ago the Rev. Stowell Brown sat in that chair, full of life, full of all the manly vigour of which he was ever characterised; and his honest, affectionate words have not, I trust, been forgotten by you. There was a cordiality expressed not only by his words but evidenced by his manner towards me in this work in which I am engaged. For the last thirty-six [sic] years his voice has been raised with no uncertain tones in the interests of the people. He spoke to them with the honest sentiments of his heart. He had a burly, manly, straightforward way with him in speaking to the people.[97]

Moving on

In the weeks that followed, the church at Myrtle Street recovered only slowly from the death of their leader, their pastor and their friend. William Caine MP, Brown's son-in-

---

[97] Ibid.

law, wrote: 'To his church and congregation the blow was stunning. He had been their faithful friend and minister for nearly forty years.'[98] But Caine also reports that his death was marked by 'the absence of a single defection, and by the continuance, with unabated energy of all the many agencies for Christian work in which he took so deep an interest'.[99] If it is true as Caine says that people did not leave Myrtle Street as a result of Brown's death that is indeed remarkable, as it was then and still is now usual for a church to have many people who are loyal to one preacher, who will go off seeking another when their favoured preacher leaves.

It took a full year for the church to find a replacement minister, and the person they found did not stay long. Rev Duncan P McPherson was a Scot from Glasgow who answered the call in 1887 to take up the mantle of the renowned Hugh Stowell Brown. Caine reports: 'He came to an earnest disciplined church, full of Christian zeal and work, whose generosity, self-sacrifice and energy have made it a society almost unique in English Non-conformity.'[100] Taking on such a church, however, was a difficult task, and he only stayed for five years. He moved to London and then on to Exeter.

The next minister at Myrtle Street could not have been more different from Hugh Stowell Brown in looks, being small and slight and clean-shaven, but was much more like

[98] W S Caine, Preface to Hugh Stowell Brown, ed W S Caine, *Extracts from His Commonplace Book*, in *Hugh Stowell Brown, A Memorial Volume*, p ix.

[99] Ibid, Preface, p ix.

[100] Ibid.

him in the ministry he offered the church. Rev John Thomas was a Welshman, born in Maesteg in South Wales in 1859. He had studied at the University of London and trained for the Baptist ministry at Pontypool Baptist College and the University College of North Wales, Bangor. He had been minister at Salendine Nook Baptist Church near Huddersfield in Yorkshire from 1884.

Like Brown, John Thomas became a well-known preacher and teacher of the Christian faith. Volumes of his sermons were published and sold well. Also like Brown, he travelled to the United States. In 1909 he was one of the speakers at the Grove City Bible Conference, a famous annual Bible conference that attracted speakers and students from all over the world, held at Grove City College near Pittsburgh, Pennsylvania.

Thomas also continued Brown's work of planting churches across Liverpool and beyond, and in 1908 Myrtle Street planted a new church in the 'new garden suburb of Wavertree', a new housing development to the south-east of the city. The church, at first called Dovedale Road Baptist Church, was for a long time called Wavertree Baptist Church, then latterly Dovedale Baptist Church. John Thomas remained as minister at Myrtle Street until 1915, and he died in 1944.

The closure of Myrtle Street chapel

By the time of his death, Myrtle Street Church was closed and the chapel demolished. During the last decade of the nineteenth century, the wealthy and influential people of Liverpool had all moved out to the southern fringes of the city or to the Wirral, and in the first decades of the twentieth century new building, such as that in Wavertree, had cleared Liverpool's city centre of most of its residential accommodation. New churches were now nearer to where people lived. In addition, the crisis of faith that came with the Great War meant church attendance declined further.

In 1939 the minister at Myrtle Street was Rev Kenneth C Dykes. Dykes was another man after the mould of Hugh Stowell Brown, a staunch Baptist with a fierce intellect, a good leader and fine preacher. But Dykes knew that it was time for Myrtle Street Church to close. In 1939 Wavertree Baptist Church, as it was then known, had no minister, and it was decided that Myrtle Street would close and Dykes would become the minister at Wavertree and the whole membership at Myrtle Street, as they were willing, would join Wavertree. In 1948 Kenneth Dykes left the church to become principal of Manchester College, now Northern Baptist College.

After the Second World War the Liverpool city planners carried out a scheme of renewal in the city centre. Liverpool had suffered greatly from aerial bombardment during the war, especially in the May blitz of 1941, but some have said that the post-war planners did more harm than the Luftwaffe to the built heritage of Liverpool, and Myrtle Street chapel was demolished as part of the clearance of redundant buildings.

Myrtle Street Baptist Church was no architectural beauty, partly because of the additions to the building made in Brown's time. But if the chapel still stood it would be partway between the city's two new cathedrals: the great neo-Gothic Anglican Cathedral of Christ and the modernist Roman Catholic Cathedral of Christ the King, as a third 'grace' on Hope Street and a city-centre focus for the Free Church community.

12
What He Believed

In many respects Hugh Stowell Brown was, as we all are, a product of his time and of his culture. He was a mainstream evangelical Baptist Christian with nineteenth-century values. What ran through his veins most of all was not his identity as a Baptist Christian but as an evangelical Christian. This he inherited from his father, who was the lowest of Low Church Anglicans.

Hugh, like, his father, was an outsider. First of all, he was not an Englishman but a Manxman. He was a man from the margins of British culture, living as member of an immigrant community in England. To look at him and to hear him speak, you would not know he was anything but an English gentleman. No one ever remarked that he spoke with a distinctive Manx accent, but he never considered himself a complete member of the English middle class; he was always an incomer.

Secondly, he never did get used to having money. Although he lived a comfortable life in an Edwardian town house with a large middle-class income, he never forgot the poverty of his childhood. As a boy his family were never as poor as the people he worked with in the slums and courthouses of Liverpool, but he lived with a sense of injustice that his father was not paid the income due to him and his mother only ever scraped a poor living. He lived his whole life with a chip on his shoulder about money.

Money, money, money

Brown's private notebook of his thoughts very often mentions his concerns about money. He frequently speaks of his annoyance at being asked for money and his unwillingness to give money to others. Then he very often corrects himself for his natural inclination to be ungenerous. On this matter we have an insight into Brown's inner life and the tension between the call to discipleship expressed in generosity and the throwback to a childhood of financial struggle and meagre living.

One private note reads, 'On Sunday I rather grudgingly gave a £5 note to the Hospital collections. I confess I had to wrestle with a temptation. The next day my wife receives from her father £50, with an intimation that she was to have as much once a quarter – £200 per annum.'[101] This comment illuminates Brown's struggle. He has given a large amount to charity, but has given it grudgingly, and then when the family has received an unexpected windfall he has felt guilty about his own lack of generosity. So his conflicted thoughts about money continued. Brown was still paid very handsomely, one of the most highly paid Free Church ministers in the country. In 1861 he was being paid an annual salary of £900 while a typical Welsh Baptist minister might be paid only £25 a year.

It is striking, reading the Myrtle Street Church minute-books, how much church business was to do with

---

[101] Ibid, p 165.

numbers. Those numbers were either the number of people being baptised or the number of members, or the number of children in Sunday school, or the number of churches being planted and cared for, or amounts of money. Money was raised for building work and money was given to numerous good causes and the salary of the pastor was always being debated. Likewise Brown's *Commonplace Book* is full of figures: how many attended the meetings he spoke at and how much he received in preaching fees.

Faithful to the gospel

Brown's inheritance from his father was not financial but it was of greater worth; it was his living faith in Jesus Christ and his love of the Bible. Brown grew up as an evangelical Christian, that is one who gave priority to the truth of the Bible and reliance on it for the life of faith. In his parents, Brown saw a simple and unadorned faith that was about taking the Bible at face value and living by its precepts. His faithful and hard-working father, who spent so many hours in study and prayer, inspired Brown to the devotional life and to preaching the simple gospel to whoever would listen.

As an evangelical, Hugh had a high view of the Bible. The faith he lived by and the faith he preached was based entirely on the Bible as he understood it. His hours of study were mainly spent in studying the text of the Bible itself, and his sermons always began from the Bible. His aim was to relate the truth of the Bible to the everyday life of his hearers.

A principle that was even more important to Hugh than evangelicalism was what the Victorians called 'voluntarism'. It was this attitude to religion that took him from the Church of England into the Baptist movement and gave him a lifelong allergy to establishment faith. Hugh was at his roots a voluntarist and an independent.

Voluntarism as a political philosophy is the belief that all relations between people should be by mutual consent and that no power should ever be forced upon anyone. So, in 1843, when parliament considered making school attendance compulsory for children who worked in factories, voluntarists were concerned – not because they opposed education but because education would be placed under the sole control of the Church of England who ran the parish schools. Voluntarism also includes the idea of personal responsibility and is more Liberal and libertarian than Socialist in its politics.

In the religious sense, voluntarism was the freedom to belong to the church of your choosing and to follow your own beliefs without coercion. In Chapter 13 of his memoirs, Brown says that the connection between Church and State was not the main issue that caused him to leave the Church of England, but that he was affected by events in Scotland, where in 1843 the Free Church of Scotland had broken from the Church of Scotland on the issue of the relation of the Church to the State. The shock waves of this 'Disruption' as it is known would have been felt more strongly in the Isle of Man than in England, and Hugh records that for him it 'raised the repute of voluntaryism and indeed induced me towards it'.[102]

---

[102] Ibid, p 63.

The issue of religious voluntarism, or what we might call the separation of Church and State, became an increasingly important issue for Brown through his life. In this he was doubtless influenced by his early mentor E L Forster, who was a member of the council of the British Anti-State-Church Association and took part in its first conference in London in 1844. When Brown went to America in 1872, he was impressed with the way the churches operated free from government intervention. In his account of the magnificence of the church buildings in America he says 'in their churches the people of the United States certainly do give a magnificent testimony to the power of voluntaryism'.[103]

Being a Baptist

Being a Baptist Christian was for Hugh Stowell Brown a natural extension of being an evangelical and a voluntarist. As a voluntarist he could not agree with the baptism of babies and the implied imposition of Christian faith and church membership upon those who had no choice. Becoming first a Dissenter and then a Baptist while training for ministry in the Church of England was explicitly a rejection of his father's position, and the impulse of a young man embracing what was important to him. The position he took before he ever joined a Baptist church remained consistent throughout his life, where he remained loyal to the Baptist cause as the home of an evangelical faith, a voluntarist philosophy and Liberal politics.

---

[103] Ibid, p 102.

A line drawing of Hugh Stowell Brown in his later years (photo: public domain)

When Brown came to sum up the progress of his own beliefs as he wrote his memoirs in 1885, he reflected on the way his reading of some great works had refined his thoughts but left the principles of his faith unchanged. He wrote that the sceptical writings he had been reading:

> do not seem to me to have shaken in the least any of the grand principles of the Gospel of Christ, while such of them as have been written in the interests of Christianity have thrown glorious light upon

Scripture, cleared up my obscurities, removed my difficulties, answered my objections, and caused the character, life, and work of Christ to appear nobler, more beautiful, and more precious than ever! And so, with some old Opinions abandoned and some others modified, I can declare after these many years, which have of course in my case included much reading and study upon religious questions, I can declare with all sincerity that the only difference in my faith in Christianity as a revelation from God, and in Christ as the Saviour of the world, is this — that it has become deeper and stronger year by year. I hope my spirit is broader and more Catholic than it was, but it is not a whit less in sympathy with what we understand by the phrase, 'Evangelical religion.'[104]

Open-minded

Although Brown stuck strongly to his convictions, he was not closed-minded in his views and not narrow in his interests. Unlike some evangelicals of his days, he developed friendships with Roman Catholics such as Monsignor James Nugent who, as we have seen, spoke warmly of Brown after his death.

Brown also expressed an affinity with Mormons, whom he saw as fellow nonconformists. In our generation, evangelical Christians generally regard the Mormon Church, more properly the Church of Jesus Christ of Latter-Day Saints, as far removed from Christian

---

[104] Ibid, p 98.

orthodoxy. In contrast Brown has some surprisingly generous encounters with Mormons. In Brown's time Mormon teaching was not the same as it is now, but it is surprising that he did not seem to know of their unbiblical teaching such as the doctrine taught at this time that identified Adam with God.[105] As noted earlier, Brown first heard a Mormon speak in Northampton while he was living in Wolverton, an American missionary who was 'haranguing' in the Market Square. Hugh records this encounter as his first attempt at public speaking. He also encountered Mormons in Liverpool and in Salt Lake City on his American trip.

Hugh was known in his time for holding unorthodox views on a subject that set him apart from most other evangelicals of his day. That was on the subject of 'annihilationism'. This doctrine, also called 'conditional immortality', is the belief that the Bible teaches that when an unbeliever dies, they face judgement and then the complete and eternal ending of their life. Immortal life is granted to the believer, but the unbeliever is not cast into hell but is separated forever from God by eternal death or 'annihilation'. This view has been held by a minority of evangelical Christians in every generation and has a resurgence in the twenty-first century through the influence of preachers such as John Stott.

Brown held this view: that there was judgement after death and judgement was based on faith in Christ and in the proper practice of faith, but that eternal punishment

---

[105] For more information on this and its connection to Brigham Young, see https://en.wikipedia.org/wiki/Adam–God_doctrine (accessed 23rd February 2019).

meant the deprivation of eternal life and fellowship with God. This teaching is only hinted at in Brown's surviving lectures and sermons. It is not mentioned at all in his memoirs or any of his obituaries or eulogies, and so was not a matter of great contention or concern. But it is referred to in some contemporary sources and was clearly known by those who listened to Brown's teaching. In the book *Here and Hereafter* by Uriah Smith,[106] Hugh Stowell Brown is cited as one of the well-known proponents of the doctrine of annihilationism in Britain, alongside the Congregational minister Joseph Parker (1830–1902) of the City Temple, London and the theologian John Bickford Heard (b 1828).

One note in the *Commonplace Book* makes reference to Brown's unorthodox views on immortality. He says:

> It is worthy of consideration whether, with all their boasted orthodoxy and evangelicalism, those who hold to the natural and necessary immortality of the soul are looking for all to Christ. They are not looking to Him for eternal life, but for that which is to make eternal life happy. Christ is not their life, but the happiness of their life.[107]

On the other hand, in another note in his *Commonplace Book*, Hugh seems to deny that he holds to this teaching:

> Today I received a letter from one of the members of the Church, demanding of me whether I hold and

---

[106] Uriah Smith, *Here and Hereafter* (Washington DC: Review and Herald Publishing, 1897).

[107] Hugh Stowell Brown, ed W S Caine, *Extracts from His Commonplace Book*, in *Hugh Stowell Brown, A Memorial Volume*, p 182.

preach the doctrine of annihilation, as if so, she must resign her membership; and as some arrangement will have to made about her pew at the end of the year, she wishes to have an answer as early as possible. I have been friendly with these people for nearly thirty years, never had a quarrel, and now for a mere false rumour they would leave. I think it is the pew-rent more than the annihilation.[108]

His comment that this is a 'false rumour' is fascinating. The weight of evidence is that he did hold to the doctrine of annihilationism, but he was careful not to preach the doctrine in his church and not base any aspect of his ministry upon it.

Brown was an evangelical but not a fundamentalist. He liked people in his church to hold a variety of views. In another place in the *Commonplace Book* he says:

At Church meeting today, C------ elected deacon, after having declared himself an open communicant and a disbeliever in particular redemption and eternal punishment. Election taking place on this declaration, and finding him at head of poll, is in effect an opening of the Church for communion, though not membership, and is a setting of the deed and its doctrines at defiance.[109]

This extract by itself is ambiguous. Is Brown concerned that a man who believed in open communion (that a person could take communion when not baptised as a

---

[108] Ibid, p 181.
[109] Ibid, p 154.

believer) and annihilationism could be elected a deacon? I think, in context, he is not. Rather he is reflecting on the changes happening in his church and broadly welcoming the liberalism they are bringing.

In an essay called 'Heresy' in the *Commonplace Book*, Brown says the charges of heresy brought against people through the history of the Christian Church have been 'dismal, disgraceful and disgusting'. He lambasts those who in the past have seen heresy as a worse crime than murder, and how in his own day 'a drunkard of evangelical views is supposed to have a better chance of salvation than the most sober man who doubts the Mosaic authorship of the Pentateuch'. He reflects that 'the heresy of one sect is the orthodoxy of another' and 'the heresy of one age is the orthodoxy of the next' and calls for people to have an independent mind. He says, 'A man is not good for much unless there be something of the heretic in him.'[110]

Restlessness with institutions

Hugh's own independent mind led him to despair of the institutions of the Church. Although he served as president of the Baptist Union and was the mainstay of many committees, he was not a man to whom institutional faith came easy.

It is worth quoting in full in this context a lengthy passage from his *Commonplace Book* about Brown's ideal church. The *Commonplace Book* is not in strict chronological order but this passage seems to be from about 1878, by which time Hugh was becoming president of the Union

---

[110] Ibid, pp 254-257.

and had been at Myrtle Street for thirty years. He had an assistant minister to help with the work. Two of his children were happily married, with a third about to be married. He had recovered from his serious illness. His wife Phoebe was well and they were living in a big house with servants. Life was as good as it would ever be. But Hugh still yearned for the perfect church:

> What I should like best would be this: - To hire a hall, e.g. Hope Hall, by the year, for Sundays, and such other times as might be agreed upon. Then there would be no bother about building, trust deed, trustees building committees, &c. And this would also be apostolical. The primitive Christians met in such places and had no buildings of their own. Then I would ask some seven men of honest report to join me and act as a committee, and the only committee, as in the Acts of the Apostles I find only one committee, consisting of seven, commonly called deacons; and I have objection to calling my seven by this name. I would have no Church. I would simply have a congregation (an Ecclesia), consisting of all who chose to come and join in worship. I would celebrate the supper of our Lord every Lord's day, morning and evening, alternately inviting all Christian friends to join, leaving it themselves, to their own consciences, to determine their fitness, and so avoiding the arrogance and presumption and inquisitorial curiosity of a Church in regard to admissions.
>
> I would baptize in the profession of their faith all those who wished to be baptized, and who satisfied me and my seven men as to character; and when

baptized, they should be just as they were, members of the congregation. I would have a meeting of the congregation once a year, to give an account of moneys, &c.

I would leave it to each member of the congregation to decide what sum he would contribute, and would supply him with accommodation as far as possible. I would have Sunday schools in private homes, Christian people lending their drawing-rooms, parlours, or kitchens for the purpose, and gathering a few children. I should have weekly offerings or collections for charities, and especially for Baptist Institutions; for my principles as a Baptist are as firm as ever. I should feel free to speak the Word of God without fear, and could be far more honest than those cramping churches allow a man to be. I should perhaps gather around me a number of intelligent, humble, peaceable, God-fearing people, whom churches have disgusted. I should have nothing to do with Liberationists and their movement but should try to cultivate Christian friendliness with all Christian people.

I think that in as large a place as Liverpool there is scope for a free and liberal institution of this kind. There are believers, as well as unbelievers, who are heartily sick of denominationalism and of church and chapel tyranny.[111]

---

[111] Ibid, pp 155-156.

A ready man

Despite his frustration with Church institutions, Hugh Stowell Brown loved the Church. He loved reading and studying in depth the history of the Christian Church. Although his education had been incomplete, he became an authority on Church history, especially the Reformation period.

But Brown remained at heart a working man with a strong work ethic and a man who identified with the working people, not with the educated elites. One note to himself written in frustration at church life reads:

> If I had a nice moderate income from independent sources, nothing would please me more, and I really think be better for me, than to become more and more a teacher of the working-classes in Liverpool. Better this than to be simply the servant of a capricious congregation. I do long for a broader life than the Baptist or any other ministry affords. God send it, and that soon![112]

Hugh Stowell Brown was a man of his time, shaped every day of his life by his Manx childhood, by the example of his Low Church father and devout mother. He never shook off the poverty of his childhood and the formative years of his youth. He emerged a man of brilliant intellect, with acute awareness to the world around him and sensitivity to the people he worked among. He had a rare gift as an observer of his times, as a writer, communicator and public speaker.

---

[112] Ibid, p 153.

A fine blend of earnestness and compassion, he takes his place among those who made Liverpool the city it is today. After his death it was said of Hugh Stowell Brown that 'the common people heard him gladly',[113] taking words that were said of Jesus in Mark 12:37 (AV). He was a true friend of the poor and for that he deserves his place on the plinth he now occupies alongside the site of Myrtle Street chapel.

But as we have seen, it was said of Brown by Henry Young[114] that he was a 'ready man' because he loved to engage with popular culture and talk to everyday people, recalling the saying of Francis Bacon that, 'Reading maketh a full man, conference a ready man, and writing an exact man.'[115] So perhaps Hugh would really have preferred to have been standing at street level for an easy conversation with those who pass by.

---

[113] Ibid, Preface, p ix.
[114] Henry Young, 'Hugh Stowell Brown as Lecturer to Liverpool Working Men, from Notes by Henry Young', in ed W S Caine, *Extracts from His Commonplace Book,* in *Hugh Stowell Brown, A Memorial Volume,* p 533.
[115] Francis Bacon, 'Of Studies' (1625), in ed John Pitcher, *The Essays* (London: Penguin Classics, 1985).

13
The Statue

Soon after the death of Hugh Stowell Brown in February 1886, a memorial tablet was installed in Myrtle Street chapel by his family. The words on this simple memorial read:

> In memory of Hugh Stowell Brown, by the grace of God pastor of this Church for 38 years. Born Aug. 10, 1823, died Feb. 24, 1886. With goodwill doing service, holding forth the word of life. To a wise teacher, a faithful friend, a loving father, this Tablet is erected by his children.

The church also, in the next two years, dedicated a number of items inside the chapel to the memory of Hugh Stowell Brown. It is noted inside the front cover of the church minute-book that the church dedicated to the memory of its late pastor four stained-glass windows on the west side of the chapel, the enlargement of the choir platform and a new communion pew.

But these memorials, seen only by those who came into the chapel, were never going to be enough to remember a man who was loved by the whole city of Liverpool. Conversations began about raising a statue in his memory. The members of his church, Myrtle Street chapel, made the decision that a statue to their late minister should be designed and displayed in front of the church. A public meeting at Liverpool Town Hall then agreed to raise £1,200 to erect a statue of Brown.

A nineteenth-century postcard showing the statue outside Myrtle Street chapel (photo: public domain)

Raising the statue

The statue was to be paid for not by the church and not by the Liverpool Corporation but by public subscription. Hugh's son-in-law William Caine in the introduction to Brown's memoirs, writing in 1888, records the sentiments of the group of which he was part who were working hard to raise the money needed to commission the statue: 'The esteem of his fellow-citizens will find expression in the public statue to be erected to his memory by their subscription.'[116]

It was important to them that the statue would belong to the people of the whole city and beyond, just as Brown had been a man whose influence had been felt far beyond the community of his own church or his own denomination. The church minute-book refers to the proposal for a statue as 'the city memorial statue in the chapel yard'. The statue was to be a memorial for the city of Liverpool, not just for the church.

A committee was set up to decide how to go ahead with the statue and, most importantly, how to raise the large amount of money that was needed to commission it. The committee was chaired by Edward Mounsey, a long-time deacon of the church who lived in Upper Parliament Street. He had previously led the group which had raised £268 to allow the pastor to go on his American trip in 1872.

The minute-book records that the total amount raised for the statue by the church committee was £511 12s 4d. It is estimated that this is the equivalent of about £42,000 today. Of this amount £250 was given by the church directly and the rest by 300 people, including £10 from the church's Workman's Bank and £20 from Edward Mounsey himself. Any other financial transactions to do with the statue have been lost so we cannot be sure if the amount raised was the total cost payable for the statue, or their contribution to the larger amount that had been agreed. To put the amount in context, Brown was receiving an annual stipend of £900 in 1865, and when Spurgeon spoke at

---

[116] Hugh Stowell Brown, ed W S Caine, *Extracts from His Commonplace Book*, in *Hugh Stowell Brown, A Memorial Volume*, Preface, p viii.

Myrtle Street in 1868 on one day, morning and evening, the church raised an offering of £250 for Spurgeon's orphanage.

The funds were raised and the statue was commissioned. It was carved from Italian Carrara marble. Carrara marble is a white high-quality marble quarried in the city of Carrara in Tuscany, Italy. It has been used since the time of ancient Rome and is the material used for the Pantheon, for Michelangelo's *David* and for Marble Arch in London.

In the opinion of Nick Roberson of Sale, Cheshire, who restored the statue, Brown's statue is 'of the finest quality of carving'. The sculptor was Francis John Williamson (1833–1920), one of the finest and best-known sculptors in Victorian Britain. Williamson was said to be Queen Victoria's favourite sculptor. In 1870 the Queen commissioned him to produce a memorial to Princess Charlotte and Prince Leopold, and many members of the royal family sat for him. In 1888 he had just completed the Jubilee bust of Queen Victoria for the Glasgow International Exhibition, which was widely copied.

The working man

The statue of Hugh Stowell Brown stands eight feet tall and weighs 2.7 tonnes without its plinth. The face on the statue is a fair likeness of Brown as he was in the last years of his life. He still has a good head of hair, just receding at the temples. The beard is a little less long than he wore it through his adult life, but his eyebrows are prominent and the nose is straight and long. He has lost some of the extra weight he carried around his cheeks in his younger years. It is clearly his face. The body likewise is in lifelike proportions.

In his statue Brown wears a four-button sack coat, done up at the top button in the usual style of the day. This was the coat of the common businessman: the shopkeeper or banker. This banking allusion is continued in what he is holding and how he is depicted. Brown is not preaching to the crowds like the famous statue of John Wesley in the grounds of St Paul's Cathedral in London. In his left hand he holds a small book. It's not a Bible but a notebook. In his right hand is not a pen but a penny. This is the statue not of Hugh Stowell Brown the preacher and lecturer, but of Brown the founder of the Workman's Bank, the preacher who worked in practical and material ways for the poor of Liverpool.

The statue is lifelike, but it is also of its time. A work strikingly similar to Williamson's Hugh Stowell Brown statue is a work of Albert Bruce-Joy in Albert Square, Manchester, of a man known to Brown, the Quaker and Liberal statesman John Bright, completed in 1891. Bright, like Brown, is standing in front of a short column draped with cloth.

The red granite plinth on which Brown's statue stood was engraved with the words: 'Hugh Stowell Brown, born 1823, died 1886. He laboured for 39 years to improve the social and spiritual condition of his fellow men.' Brown would have approved of most of the details of that wording. He would have been pleased that his name is not recorded as 'Rev Hugh Stowell Brown' for he had no time for titles. He would have enjoyed the word 'laboured', because he saw his work as laborious in the sense of careful and exact and also as hard work. He liked to see himself as a labourer for the gospel. He would also like the reference to 'his fellow men' because he saw himself as a man of the people, in no way above the people whom he served. One phrase he might have questioned is 'improve the social and spiritual condition'. He might have thought that the spiritual should come before the social and that only God could improve people's spiritual condition. Overall, though, Brown would not have been unhappy with the words with which the city has been left to remember him.

A public tribute

On its completion the statue was installed outside the front door of Myrtle Street chapel, just behind the church railings next to the pavement. The statue was unveiled at a ceremony led by the Myrtle Street chapel leaders and the city officials on Tuesday 15th October 1889. The statue stood facing the side of the old Philharmonic Hall, a grand, imposing building which opened in 1849 and burned down in 1933.

There is another public memorial to Hugh Stowell Brown in Liverpool, very close to where the statue originally stood, which still remains in its original location. Just a few yards up Hope Street from where Myrtle Street chapel stood there is a road named 'Stowell Street' that is named after Hugh Stowell Brown. It was originally a backstreet without a name that had dwellings built on it and needed to be given a name. It was given the name Stowell Street without reference to Brown and without his consent. Brown mentions it in his *Commonplace Book* in passing in an entry from about 1875. He says:

> The Vaughans have launched a new ship and called her the 'Stowell Brown'. This is an honour very rarely conferred upon a minister. But, *per contra*, a very small mean street next to the Lying-in Hospital is called Stowell Street – I think with reference to me.[117]

Brown is much less impressed with the 'very small mean street' than with a ship launched with his name, but it is the street name that has survived. Stowell, was, of course, Brown's middle name, a given name, not part of his surname. But he always called himself 'Hugh Stowell Brown' and often signed his named 'H Stowell Brown' and Stowell was and is still taken by many to be part of his family name, and the reason why a street named after him is named after his middle Christian name.

The statue stood outside Myrtle Street for more than fifty years, through two world wars, and through the closure of the chapel. But when the chapel was to be demolished, the statue had to be moved. Technically it belonged to no one. It didn't belong to the city, and it didn't belong to the church. The money had been raised by a church committee by public subscription. As the chapel was demolished to make way for new city-centre developments, the Liverpool Corporation put the statue into storage for a few years until it was decided where it should go next.

---

[117] Ibid, p 162.

The statue moved and lost, and found

On Saturday 25th September 1954 the statue and its original plinth were moved to a new home. The new site for the statue was on Princes Avenue in Liverpool 8, outside Princes Gate Baptist Church, a church founded by Brown and the people of Myrtle Street in 1881.

The empty plinth in Princes Avenue in 2009 (photo: Wayne Clarke)

After the demolition of the Princes Gate Church in 1974, the statue remained on a strip of grassland in the middle of the road in Toxteth that is called Princes Road on one side and Princes Avenue on the other, and opposite the gates of Princes Park. On the other end of this strip another statue had been placed, a statue to William Huskisson, the Liverpool MP and first man ever killed on the railways in 1830.

The statue survived the Toxteth riots of 1981 and further disturbances in 1985 when damage was done to the built environment in the immediate area around the Princes Park gates. But in 1988 the statue of Huskisson was toppled from its plinth. It has been said that a small group of people attacked the Huskisson statue thinking that he was a slave trader – which he was not – and then started targeting the Brown statue for the same erroneous reason. The Liverpool authorities took evasive action and removed the statue of Hugh Stowell Brown, leaving the plinth behind, at the same time as removing the statue of Huskisson.

For many years the statue seemed to be forgotten and was lost from public memory. In Dovedale Baptist Church the memory of Brown persisted through a project that had been begun by their minister Rev Mark Rudall and continued by the present author. Mark Rudall had produced a series of pictures telling the story of Hugh Stowell Brown and this raised my curiosity about his life, his legacy and the location of his statue. Through the privilege of working for the BBC in Liverpool I was able to gain access to people within Liverpool City Council. These people at first had no knowledge of the statue and declared it lost. But I persisted and in 2007 I tracked down one man who thought he remembered what had happened to the statue back in 1988.

I arranged a meeting with this council officer and showed him a photograph of the statue as it had stood in Princes Road and this sparked in him a glimmer of recognition. He took me to Croxteth Country Park, a large council-owned public park on the edge of Liverpool. Within the country park we went to Croxteth Farm, an appropriately Victorian working farm in the grounds of Croxteth Hall, formerly part of Lord Sefton's estate.

Around the back of the farm, well out of the public areas, we found a series of stable yards, used for waste products, storage and derelict vehicles. We entered one of these yards and walked through a trail of discarded old farm machinery. And there, lying in a corner, against a rough brick wall and some old fencing, was the forlorn but recognisable figure of Hugh Stowell Brown.

It was clear to my untrained eyes that the statue had suffered serious damage. The lower front parts of the sack coat were broken. Both hands were missing. The face was badly eroded. But it was clearly the same statue that had stood in front of his chapel after his death and then in front of Princes Gate Church for many years after. The statue was found and had to be restored.

The broken statue lying forgotten in Croxteth Farm stable yard, 2007 (photo: Wayne Clarke)

The statue restored

The discovery of the statue was brought to the public's notice through BBC Radio Merseyside and the work of David Charters of the *Liverpool Daily Post*, who did as much as anyone to start a campaign to get the statue restored. The initial campaign was spearheaded by the Friends of Liverpool Monuments Civic Society.

The first job was to prevent any further damage by moving the statue away from the harm that was being done to it in its Croxteth farmyard. Liverpool City Council showed willing and at one point nearly funded the restoration, but then a change of political leadership within the council put a stop to that.

It was not until 2013 that a financial solution was found when a development company called Nordic Construction wanted to build student apartments on the exact site where Myrtle Street Baptist Church had formerly stood. For years the site had been a car park, but it was a prime site for accommodation for the growing student population of Liverpool. A deal was stuck that as part of the student development the company should finance the restoration and re-siting of the Hugh Stowell Brown statue on Hope Street at the entrance to the apartments and opposite the Philharmonic pub. It was an inspired idea: to reclaim for the site a link with its history and use the potential that lay in the land to restore the memory of its greatest tenant, just around the corner from where the statue originally stood.

The restoration was to be coordinated by sculptor Nick Roberson of Roberson Stone Carving and Stewart Darlow of Nordic Construction to ensure the project was kept as original as possible. Nick Roberson visited the statue in

Croxteth to examine and evaluate the damage and saw more than I had done some seven years previously.

Nick Roberson himself continues the story of the highly skilled and painstaking job of restoration:

> I examined it at Croxteth and it was missing both hands, both ears, nose, left foot and most of the delicate front of the frock coat. The worst damage in many ways was caused before the riots by the sandblast cleaning probably done in the early 1980s which removed much of the lavish detail that would have originally been there.
>
> The extensive restoration began with cleaning the once white marble. This included removal of lichen, algae and moss and extensive steam cleaning. The hands, foot and frock coat damage were replaced using matching Italian marble and original photographic reference to replicate the lost detail. This left the nose and ears which were restored using marble dust and lime in accordance with current accepted restoration practice.
>
> I was only permitted to clean the stone with mild chemicals and steam as anything else may further damage the piece. This sadly left some dark and deep lichen stains and a faint yellow colour over the whole sculpture. This yellowing was due to the sulphur present in coal smog which turned this sculpture (and every building in the city) black over the years until its cleaning some time during the '70s or '80's.
>
> After extensive cleaning I sculpted new hands in clay and fixed them temporarily on to the sleeves and compared the original photograph of the pre-

damage statue with one taken in the workshop to compare the size and form of the hands. Once satisfied, I copied the clay hands in new marble. This was painstaking but the only way to ensure an accurate replacement of the missing elements. This was also true of the foot and coat details.

The nose and ears were 'restored' using lime repair in accordance with English Heritage guidelines. The coat details were difficult as the hem of the garment was only very thin and the new marble was attached with stainless dowels at times only 2mm from the surface when carving was finished.

The sculpture was then coated with a marble dust and lime slurry to blend the old stone with the new repairs. I was surprised by the finished result as during cleaning I began to forget just how dark and sad it was originally.[118]

Nick Roberson is to be commended for the fine job he has done. The restoration of the statue has been completed magnificently and the statue has been returned to the way it was first seen by William and Alice Caine, Edward Mounsey, Hugh's family and those who knew him best. Although there are still signs of wear, the statue is recognisably the image of Hugh Stowell Brown and still captures the man in his later years standing confidently with his generous, open stance.

---

[118] Nick Roberson, letter to the author, 7th August 2016.

The restored statue in Hope Street, Liverpool plate (photo: Rev Dr
David Steers, velvethummingbee.wordpress.com, used by permission)

Back where he belongs

On 10th September 2015 the restored statue and original plinth were finally reunited and erected on Hope Street. The statue stands close to another statue remembering the partnership of two more recent Liverpool church leaders, Bishop David Sheppard and Archbishop Derek Worlock by Stephen Broadbent. It forms part of what David Sheppard called the *Steps Along Hope Street*,[119] on a direct line between Liverpool's two great cathedrals, emphasising the essential unity of the work of service that the Christian Church offers to the city.

With the return of the statue, the story of Hugh Stowell Brown is complete, and his memory will remain in Liverpool city centre for years to come. His legacy will only linger, though, if the work to which he was committed continues to be done among each new generation of Christians and other people of goodwill, people who seek to bring goodness and godliness into the city of Liverpool and into the world.

---

[119] David Sheppard, *Steps along Hope Street: My Life in London and Liverpool* (London: Hodder & Stoughton, 2003).

Appendix
Penny Wise and Pound Foolish[120]

There is in the world a good deal of false economy, which turns out in the end to be great and ruinous extravagance. There are many people who believe that they are laying out time, and money, and effort to the best advantage, when in reality they are squandering them in the most wasteful manner possible. There are many old sayings which illustrate this mistake, and put us on our guard against it. For example: 'To lose a ship for a halfpenny worth of tar;' 'To spare at the spigot, and let out at the bunghole;' 'For want of a nail the shoe was lost, for want of a shoe the horse was lost, for want of a horse the rider was lost;' to which I add, as the shortest and most exact description of the error which we are about to discuss, the proverb, which I have chosen as the motto of this lecture, 'Penny Wise and Pound Foolish'. The conduct indicated by these proverbs is far from uncommon. There are some people who are both penny foolish and pound foolish, or rather, who are so foolish with their pennies, that they never have pounds to be foolish with at all; people who have no notion whatever of economy and thrift, who live from hand to mouth, and, whenever they get money, spend it with the utmost

---

[120] Originally published in Hugh Stowell Brown, ed R Shelton Mackenzie, *Lectures for the People*, pp 127-144.

possible despatch. For such folk this lecture is not intended; the penny foolish I must for the present leave in their folly. I wish to speak to the penny wise and to guard them, if I can, against the mistake of becoming pound foolish; I wish to speak to those who really have some idea of saving and economical habits, but who very possibly mistake the cheap for the dear, and the dear for the cheap, and so lose all the benefits of their industry and their toil.

Sometimes we find 'the penny wise and pound foolish' principle illustrated on a very large scale by Government. The 'collective wisdom', hereditary and elected, often shows itself to be but a 'penny wisdom', saving a little and losing much. For example: it makes something in the Excise department, by licensing such a multitude of beer-houses; but every man must be perfectly aware that the loss to the country, arising from the intemperance, the idleness, and the extravagance nurtured by the beer-house, is immeasurably greater than the entire amount which the Excise yields to the revenue. For while the money loss is great, this is the smallest of comfort, there is a loss of industry, there is moral deterioration, there is ignorance, there is brutishness, there is crime – all encouraged, all to a great extent produced, by the beer-house system. Then think of the paper duty; I believe it returns to the Government a little more than a million, in hard cash; but it is a heavy tax upon the spread of knowledge, upon the communication of thought; it interferes with the mental and moral culture of the people; we put down to its credit a million; if we could put to its credit ten millions, there would be a heavy balance against it, in the fact that it is a barrier to national enlightenment, and therefore most injurious to national morals – a most flagrant case of 'penny wise and pound foolish,' and one which it is to be hoped public opinion will soon compel Government to correct.

And now to come to another, but not unimportant, illustration of our motto. I would observe that many people are 'penny wise and pound foolish' in the matter of educating their children. Very often boys are taken from school just at the time when they are really beginning to learn something, when they are capable of making progress, and when the rudimentary instruction of earlier years has prepared them to advance. At the age of twelve or thirteen they can earn a trifle of money, earn possibly enough to keep themselves in food and clothing. In some of the manufacturing districts they can be set to work much earlier; and I have seen little things of six or seven years cooped up in hot and dusty rooms, and kept there until seven or eight o'clock at night, to the ruin of their health, as well as the impoverishment of their minds. Of course there is a temptation, and, when parents are very poor, a strong temptation, to compel children to earn their own bread as soon as possible. But it is very false economy to do so; it places an almost insurmountable barrier in the way of a lad's advancement in the world. A wise parent therefore will, I think, do all in his power, and, if need be, make great sacrifices, to keep his children at school beyond the years of mere infancy. Out of school, that boy of twelve could earn perhaps three shillings a-week; but don't suppose that in school he is earning nothing. There, if the school and the boy himself be good for anything, he is earning what is worth a great deal more than three shillings a-week; he is furnishing himself with that knowledge which must be his capital when he enters on the business of life. So much arithmetic learned every week, so much geography, so much history, so much geometry, algebra, natural philosophy, grammar – all this, earned every week, is worth a great deal more than the three shillings which he could get as an errand-boy. To deprive him of all this, is to make a terrible sacrifice, is certainly to act in the 'penny wise and pound foolish' style. Therefore, if you can avoid it, do so; if, by means of any self-denial, you can keep your son at school until he reaches the age of fifteen, you will have no reason to regret the exercise of such self-denial, you will be amply repaid for it. Even if he should not live to profit by his education, or if, through his misconduct in after-life, he should disappoint all your hopes, still you will have the consciousness of having discharged your duty to him, of having done your best to make him a prosperous, useful, and respectable man.

Sometimes the 'penny wise and pound foolish' principle is exhibited in the choice which people make of a place to dwell in. All our large towns, and this town certainly as much as any other, abound in houses — if houses they can be called — which are not fit to be the abodes of beasts, but are, nevertheless, densely inhabited by men, women, and children. The problem, how to crowd the largest number of human beings into the smallest possible space, has been as triumphantly solved by our architects and builders, as by our grave-diggers. The narrow, dark, unventilated, undrained, unwholesome, dwellings of the poor are a reproach to us, a shame and a misery to behold; all that municipal authorities and boards of health can do is unavailing to make these wretched abodes as healthy as they ought to be; they are, and they must be, the haunts of pestilence and death. There are some whose unavoidable poverty leaves them no other resource than to shelter themselves in such abominable kennels; there are others whose intemperance prevents their obtaining better homes; there are many whose love of dirt leads them to prefer these tumble-down hovels. But an industrious man who can earn tolerably good wages need not imprison himself there; it is very false economy for him to do so; the cheap and nasty house is dear at any price. When a good commodious house in a healthy part of the town, or in the suburbs, is to be let, it is generally advertised in terms which set forth all its advantages, and in which the truth, and even a good deal more than the truth, is told respecting it. I should like to see an advertisement which should deal faithfully with another class of habitations. It would be to the following effect:

'To be let, immediately, a house, situated in the most insalubrious locality within a circuit of fifty miles; this most eligible dwelling forms a part of a court, exactly two yards and a half wide; it is so well sheltered that neither light nor air can reach it; it is destitute of all the conveniences and decencies of life; in its construction the utmost care has been taken to render it in all respects as injurious to health as possible. The house is largely stocked with various kinds of vermin, and the neighbourhood is celebrated for its bad smells and stagnant gutters. The landlord is prepared to prove that the premises have not been cleaned for the last eighteen years; the last tenant buried four of his children in the space of six months, from which it will be seen that it is a highly desirable residence for a man with a large and burdensome family. Amongst the advantages which the above premises command, it may be stated that there are nine gin-shops within fifty yards of the door, three pawn-brokers on the opposite side of the street, and a coffin maker's establishment just round the corner. The society also is very select – there being, on an average, two man-fights and five woman-fights every week, with other agreeable entertainments to vary the monotony of existence. N.B. – There is no gas-light in the court, and no Bobby has been known to venture into it for many months.'

'Penny wise and pound foolish', I think, to live in a house like that, if you can avoid it. Unless indeed you are particularly desirous of injuring your health, and shortening your children's lives.

An extra florin or half-crown a week, where a working man can possibly spare it, is not thrown away, but right well and wisely spent in securing a clean healthy comfortable house, where there are good sewerage, good air, daylight and a plentiful supply of cold water, and where the decencies of life can be observed. Of course, however good a house is, and in however healthy a situation, it may be comfortless, and comfortless it will be – dirty, disorderly, unhealthy, in all respects miserable —if not managed aright; but still, the most careful internal arrangements will avail little, if the house and its situation are bad; and I believe that many a working man's wife, who in a decent house would keep things all tidy, is so discouraged by the difficulty of keeping a bad house in a bad neighbourhood decent, that she gives the task up in despair. By all means, if possible, let her have a house, and not a den, a sty, to keep clean, otherwise, what is saved in rent by taking this beastly hovel, will be lost in other ways; and therefore I would respectfully urge upon working men to obtain the very best habitations they can afford, since bad houses are injurious to health and to morals too. It is very hard to be good anywhere, but it is especially hard to be good in a house which by its construction and its situation is of necessity dark, dirty, and unwholesome. I do not say that if the wretched, drunken, dissolute inhabitants of some of our courts and alleys could be transported to some district containing well-built, airy, cheerful, healthy houses, they would be altogether converted by the change, but I do believe that they would be very greatly altered for the better – that they would become more susceptible of good impressions – that they would be far more likely to become virtuous and godly people, more likely to listen to the Gospel, and more likely to live the Gospel; certainly their bodily health would be improved, their lives would be lengthened, their children's morals would not be so exposed to corrupting influences; and, altogether, I do most thoroughly believe that good dwellings would go very far towards improving the character and condition of the people in almost every respect. It is a matter of thankfulness to see that the attention of good men is turned to this subject, and that efforts are being made to furnish the working people with comfortable houses; but the working people themselves must second those efforts, by doing all in their power to encourage the building of the right sort of habitations – by being prepared to take them, even though they should cost a trifle more than the dirty pest-houses, the living tombs, of the dark and narrow courts.

The 'penny wise and pound foolish' principle is often illustrated by the system on which many people act in almost all their purchases. I have often spoken of the rage for cheap things, which seems to be the order of the day. Under the shelter of this word 'cheap,' the vilest trash, in food, in drink, in clothing, in furniture, in implements, is sold in enormous quantities. Perhaps there is not a more delusive word in our language, for, generally speaking, the cheapness of an article is the result of deterioration; in proportion to its cheapness, is its nastiness, its worthlessness. What you buy dirt cheap, usually is dirt. I have heard of a gentleman who went into a great clothing establishment in London, and bought himself a suit, at a remarkably low figure. He was delighted with his purchase, and next morning sallied forth for his office in the city, dressed in his new toggery, and pleased to observe how well it fitted him, and how becoming it was in all respects; but he had not proceeded far, when first one seam and then another gave way; in a few minutes he was in rags and was compelled to take refuge in a cab, and be driven back in confusion to his lodgings, convinced that he for one had been 'penny wise and pound foolish'.

In one way or another, I dare say we have all of us made a discovery of the folly which prompts people to patronise the dirt-cheap system. It is always the most expensive in the long run – for a good article will always command a good price; and that which is very low in figure, proclaims itself low in quality as well; and many of the things that are paraded before the gaping public as extraordinarily cheap, would really be very dear at any price.

I often see advertisements headed 'Great Bargains!' What am I to make of such an announcement?, for a bargain may be good or bad. Our friend who bought the clothes which fell to tatters in the street, had a very great bargain, but a great bad one. If the advertisement were headed 'good bargains', there would be some sense in it; though even then it would remain to be decided whether the good bargain was on the side of the customer or of the shopkeeper, and I incline to think it is generally in favour of the latter; at all events, in this puffing age, when, of a multitude of shopkeepers, every one declares that his is the best and cheapest house in the trade, that his stock is unrivalled in the world, that he is selling off to make alterations in the premises, and that such an opportunity seldom presents itself, &c, it may be well to remember our old proverb, lest, enticed and tempted by such promises, and by the fine appearance which, by various artful dodges, is given to every vile piece of trumpery, and especially to the vilest, we should discover, when too late, that we have been 'penny wise and pound foolish.'

I often see this pound folly and penny wisdom in the salaries given to servants. It is a point with many people to get a person to do this or that work at as low a remuneration as possible, and the consequence often is that the work is badly done. Sometimes the salary is so small that the poor recipient of it is tempted to act dishonestly, and abscond with his master's money, taking ten times the amount of his salary at a slap. It is not a good system; it is not profitable; it is not safe; it is not creditable. Where a man does his work well, I should think the surest plan is to encourage him, by dealing with him in a generous, and not in a niggardly spirit. It may often be in a servant's power to promote or to injure his employer's interest, and therefore it is well to identify the interests of both as far as practicable. Scripture says, 'The instruments […] of [a] churl are evil;'[121] which I would venture to interpret very freely thus: the servants of a churl are not persons to be depended upon; 'but the liberal deviseth liberal things, and by liberal things shall he stand.' Liberal treatment is not thrown away upon 'the right man in the right place;' it will pay best in the long run; it will save a man from bunglers, from idlers, and from rascals (a very desirable salvation I should think); it will make him quiet and easy in his mind, and relieve him of a thousand anxieties and fears, if he knows that he has really made it worth a good man's while to serve him diligently and well. And men of the right stamp are not to be picked up any day, at any street corner; they are so difficult to find, that it is of no small consequence to keep them when you have found them. Of course there are higher principles than that of mere self-interest, which ought to prompt an employer to deal liberally with those in his employ; but, to take it on the lowest ground, it is for his own interest to act thus. What he might save in wages by employing persons of an inferior mental and moral standing, he will lose in other

---

[121] See Isaiah 32:7, AV.

ways; he will probably lose far more, and find, to his sorrow, that, in dealing with clerks, with craftsmen, with foremen, with captains and officers of ships – with the employed in all departments of business – there is such a mistake, and a costly mistake, too, as being 'penny wise and pound foolish'.

We see this error very frequently and very miserably illustrated in the investment of money. By dint of long and severe struggling, a man is enabled at last to save something. It has cost him much self-denial and much care. 'Penny wise' he certainly has been – adding by little and little to his store; and now, what is he to do with it? A hundred schemes present themselves, all very plausible – all promising a safe and large return – all demonstrating ten, fifteen, twenty, or thirty per cent, as certain. There are snares formed to entrap the wasteful, thoughtless, prodigal man; and to rob him at once, before he has accumulated as much as a week's wages in hand: there are also snares, more cunningly devised, to entrap the industrious and the thrifty; and, consequently multitudes of such persons have had every stiver [a low-value coin] cruelly swept away, and have passed their old age in poverty and want, rendered all the more bitter by the reflection that their suffering is the result of their credulity, in trusting to the flattering tales of scheming scoundrels. It is difficult to know what to advise, unless we give this one counsel — that in proportion to the return that is promised, the scheme is to be suspected. The swindling speculations are always the most brilliantly coloured — always have a most plausible appearance, and hold out the most attractive bait. It is better to leave speculation to the men who can afford to lose money; those who have to depend upon a little should try to be content with a small but certain return, and should run none of the risks which a great percentage usually involves. At all events, there are only too many sorrowful facts which prove that, after all a man's penny wisdom in making a little money by honest industry and economical habits, he may be the deluded victim of pound folly in the choice of an investment for his savings. 'All is not gold that glitters' in the speculating world; nay, I should say the more glittering there is, the less gold in general. There is an old saying, to the effect that 'if you take care of the pence, the pounds will take care of themselves.' Seldom do we meet with a more foolish proverb; the pounds require even more care than the pence, because they are more sought after by the crafty, there are greater temptations offered for their unsafe investment.

But now I shall suppose the case of a man who has fallen into none of those 'penny wise and pound foolish' mistakes which I have described. He has not been tempted by the trifle of money his sons could earn, to remove them from school so early as to spoil the process of their education, and unfit them for making advancement in the world; he has not risked his own health, and that of his family, by living in a dark, dirty and unwholesome house; he has not, for the sake of a low rent, submitted to the abominations of a vile dwelling and a vile neighbourhood; he has not been deluded by the plausible word cheap, but wisely regards the Cheap John as the dearest of all tradesmen, and suspects that a great bargain is a great thief; he has not been so foolish as to adopt the niggardly policy with those in his employ, but, with a true knowledge of human nature, has secured to himself good servants, by paying them well; nor has he been taken in by any of the swindling speculations of the age. Whatever he has put his hand to has prospered; in large transactions equally as in small, he has evinced prudence, knowledge, sagacity, and success has crowned all his efforts in life. Penny wise, and pound wise, too, he seems to be; and everyone has the highest opinion of his practical good sense. Well, after all, he may only be penny wise; he may be to the fullest extent, and in the most important sense, pound foolish; for this proverb refers not to money alone. Every man is 'penny wise and pound foolish' who is wise in the smaller affairs of life, and foolish in the greater and the greatest. If the acquisition and wise investment of money were the principal thing for which a man exists, then such a paragon of success might be regarded as a paragon of wisdom; but whether men will believe it or not, the acquisition and the investment of money, however wise and profitable the investment be, really is not the main design of our existence in this world; and I think that I can show that this model man of business, though penny wise, which I am by no means inclined to deny, is pound foolish after all, and pound foolish perhaps in several respects.

For, suppose that in his intense application to business he has injured his health, and this is no uncommon case; there are many who, in their great anxiety to prosper in the world, undermine their constitution, sow the seeds of fatal disease, and bring themselves to a premature grave. To act thus is, I think, to show oneself 'penny wise and pound foolish'. Such a man is penny wise, for he makes money;

but he is certainly pound foolish, inasmuch as he incapacitates himself for the enjoyment of the fortune which he is so intent upon realising. Or, suppose that a man's thoughts are so engrossed by his money-making schemes, that he has neither time nor inclination to think of anything else. He sacrifices all mental improvement, all acquisition of knowledge, all intellectual pleasures to his one great object – that of becoming a rich man. I should think that in that case also he must be pronounced 'penny wise and pound foolish'; he is preferring the less to the greater; he may wax very wealthy, but if he continues an ignorant creature, insensible to all refined enjoyments, deliberately devoting himself to the business of a miser, until he can find pleasure in nothing else, he is just making a fool of himself, with all his apparent shrewdness. He is penny wise, but there is no coin that can express the magnitude of his folly. If, moreover, this his greediness of gain has hardened his heart, and made him indifferent to all but himself, a close-fisted, hard-bargain-driving man, near, niggardly, and mean, so that he is feared by his dependents, hated by his equals, despised by his superiors, so that nobody has any reason to love him, to respect him, to care whether he lives or dies, – for he has made no sorrowful heart glad, relieved no wretchedness, done no good in the world, – then I think that his penny wisdom has ripened into pound folly. Still more is this the case if his thirst for gain has prevailed over his moral principles, and led him into crooked and dishonest paths, and general worship of the devil, and if, in taking such mighty care of his secular interest, he has altogether neglected his soul.

I read in Scripture this description of a man 'penny wise and pound foolish' – 'The ground of a certain rich man brought forth plentifully[. A]nd he thought within himself, saying, What shall I do, because I have no room where to bestow my fruits? And he said, This will I do[,] I will pull down my barns, and build greater[,] and there will I bestow all my fruits and my goods. And I will say to my soul, Soul, thou hast much goods laid up for many years[,] take thine ease, eat, drink, and be merry. And God said unto him, Thou fool, this night [shall thy soul] be required of thee[, and] then whose shall those things be[,] which thou hast provided? So is he that layeth up treasure for himself, and is not rich toward God.'[122] There are many such men, men careful, prudent, saving, with regard to the present life, whose selfishness culminates at last, and reaches its climax in utter neglect of themselves. It is curious to think that a man will exercise the utmost anxiety to have all his property carefully handed over to his relatives and friends; nothing is omitted, nothing left to take its chance; from his landed estate, worth one hundred thousand pounds, to his old boots not worth ninepence, every item of his property is willed this way or that; but as to his soul's future welfare, and what is to become of that, he feels not the slightest concern. This, I submit, is the very extreme form of the 'penny wise and pound foolish' principle, especially if the man is not an infidel, but a person who does believe in a judgment to come.

I have heard of a millionaire who, on his death bed, was entreated by a friend to leave some money to build two or

---

122 Luke 12:16-21, AV.

three churches for the benefit of the town in which he had risen from the very sweepings. 'Churches!' exclaimed the expiring old wretch. 'Build churches! Why, I have several pews already that are not let.' The last days of misers are indeed fearfully illustrative of our motto, 'Penny wise and pound foolish'. In fact, however shrewd, however keen, however successful a man may be in life, and however intellectual in his tastes and pursuits, however extensively and accurately informed he may be, in any case indifference to religion proves him to be but 'penny wise and pound foolish'. Another of the sayings of Him who spake as never man had spoken before, or has spoken since, will set this matter in a clear light at once: 'What shall it profit a man, if he [should] gain the whole world, and lose his own soul?'[123] To argue upon this question would be absurd; all, without a moment's hesitation pronounce that the only answer that can be given to it is this, that such gain, at such a cost, would be a dead and unutterable loss, a shocking bad bargain for any man, a most flagrant case of 'penny wise and pound foolish'. Yes, that's what everybody says – everybody, excepting perhaps an infidel, whose infidelity goes so far as to deny the immortality, perhaps to deny even the existence, of the soul. All but he at once exclaim, This question admits of but one answer — to gain the world, and lose the soul, would be to the uttermost unprofitable. I only wish that all men acted in accordance to this conviction, but what do we see? Why, this; that, not for so tempting a bribe as the whole world,

---

123 Mark 8:36, AV.

but for some poor infinitesimal fraction of the world, men exchange their souls.

One runs the risk of losing his soul, rather than not gratify his lust; another runs the risk of losing his soul, rather than abstain from excess in strong drink; and another says, Let me have money, and my soul may take its chance. When I consider for what a paltry amount of gratification some men lose their souls, I cannot call them even penny wise. I do not know of any coin, in any currency, small enough, worthless enough, to be the representative of their wisdom; nor did ever a piece of gold come from any mint large enough to express their folly. Not penny wise and pound foolish, not even farthing wise, but more than a thousand-pound foolish, are such men. The devil is very shabby in the bargains which he makes with these poor fools; he would not give Judas Iscariot more than thirty pieces of silver for his soul, and he has bought many a man for less. If he gave them a pretty large share of the world, and of worldly enjoyment; if he gave them riches, and health to enjoy them; pleasures, and a physical constitution to resist their debilitating effects: even then it would be a miserably losing game, to jeopardise the soul for one moment for such a consideration; but poverty, and ill-health, and weakness, and shame, and shortness of days are more generally the wages of sin even in this world; the fact is, it is not a question of gaining the world and losing your soul – you won't gain it. Christ asks, What shall it profit a man, if he [...] gain the whole world?[124] but he knew full well that

---

[124] Ibid.

the whole world cannot be gained, that the sinner gains but a poor little morsel of it with all his striving; and for this little morsel of the world, what a fool a man must be to imperil his future, to run the risk of eternal and irreparable loss! And it is not the miser alone who is doing this, but every man who prefers the pleasures of sin, of any kind of sin, to a sober, righteous, and godly life.

And now will you each ask yourselves, Am I in any respect 'penny wise and pound foolish?' There are many other ways of fulfilling this character besides those which I have pointed out; but what I have mentioned are common specimens, common illustrations of the principle. If we are parents, let us not be 'penny wise and pound foolish' in the treatment of our children, and their training for life. If we are poor, still let us not be 'penny wise and pound foolish' in dwelling in houses unfit for human habitation, if we can possibly dwell in better. In all our marketings and purchases let us be on our guard, lest the delusion of apparent and so-called cheapness betray us into a 'penny wise and pound foolish' outlay of money. If we are employers, let us not illustrate this treacherous principle in our treatment of those whom we engage to work for us. If we have been enabled to save anything by our toil, let us be careful, lest 'penny wise and pound foolish' investments rob us of our hard-earned treasure. Above all, may we shun that penny wisdom and pound folly, that minimum of wisdom and maximum of folly, which prefers sin to holiness, time to eternity, earth to heaven, and the body to the soul.

Bibliography

Hugh Stowell Brown, A Memorial Volume
Including his *Notes of my Life* and *Extracts from His Commonplace Book*
Ed W S Caine MP
London: George Routledge and Sons, 1888

Lectures to Working Men
Hugh Stowell Brown
London: Frederick Pitman, 1870

Lectures for the People
Hugh Stowell Brown
Philadelphia, PA: G G Evans, 1859

Our Heritage: The Baptists of Yorkshire, Lancashire and Cheshire 1647–1987
Ed Ian Sellars
The Yorkshire Baptist Association and the Lancashire and Cheshire Baptist Association, 1987

A History of English Baptists
A C Underwood
London: The Baptist Union Publication Department, 1947

The Baptist Churches of Lancashire
Ed A H Stockwell
London: Arthur H Stockwell, 1911

A History of British Baptists
W T Whitley
London: Charles Griffin and Co, 1923

Here and Hereafter, or Man in Life and Death
Uriah Smith
Washington, DC: Review and Herald Publishing Association, 1897

American Travellers in Liverpool
Ed David Seed
Liverpool: Liverpool University Press, 2008

Hugh Stowell Brown Timeline

	1822	Birth of Alice Chibnall Sirrett
10th August	1823	Hugh Stowell Brown born in Douglas
	1824	Brother John dies
5th May	1830	Birth of brother Thomas Edward Brown
	1830	Christening ceremony
	1832	Family move to Kirk Braddan
	1834	Starts to read to his father every afternoon
20th June	1837	Victoria accedes to the throne of the United Kingdom
July-September	1838	Birth of Phoebe Caine in Liverpool
6th/7th January	1839	Great storm
19th February	1839	Leaves IoM, goes to Biddulph to join Tithe Commutation Survey
January	1840	Land surveying in Harborne, Birmingham
May	1840	Leaves Birmingham and went home
June	1840	Ordnance Survey in Manchester and York

August	1840	Engineer with London & Birmingham Railway in Wolverton
December	1841	Visits London
December	1843	Leaves L&BR to study at home in Kirk Braddan
10th January	1844	Myrtle Street Baptist Church, Liverpool, opened for worship
August	1844	Begins studies at King William's College in Castletown
June	1846	Leaves King William's College
August	1846	Leaves home again, goes to Crewe, Manchester, Stony Stratford
November	1846	Baptised at Stony Stratford by Mr Forster
November	1846	Called home to Kirk Braddan, brothers Robert and Harry die
28th November	1846	Father dies chasing after Hugh on a stormy night
29th November	1846	Hears Dr Raffles preach at Great George Street Chapel, Liverpool
3rd December	1846	Father's funeral, leaving wife and seven children
January	1847	Mother and family move to Castletown
27th March	1847	Goes to Liverpool following invitation to preach

28th March	1847	Preaches at Myrtle Street Church morning and evening
4th April	1847	Preaches again at Myrtle Street Church morning and evening
August	1847	Accepts three-month trial as pastor of Myrtle Street Church
November	1847	Accepts pastorate of Myrtle Street Baptist Church
1st January	1848	Begins as the pastor of Myrtle Street church
1st March	1848	Ordained to pastoral office at Myrtle Street church
9th May	1848	Marries Alice Chibnall Sirrett at Stony Stratford Baptist Church
Feb/March	1849	Birth of daughter, Alice (first child)
	1849	Mill Street mission opened
April	1850	Birth of son, Robert (second child)
30th March	1851	Living at 9 South Myrtle St with Alice and two children
May	1851	Side galleries added to Myrtle Street
16th August	1851	Death of son, Robert, aged sixteen months
	1851	Birth of son, Hugh Stowell (third child)
23rd November	1851	Death of Rev James Lister, previous pastor

25th & 27th Oct	1853	Delivers lecture, 'The Pilgrim Fathers', at the Concert Hall
	1853	Birth of son John Sirett Brown (fourth child)
1st May	1854	Begins Sunday lectures at the Concert Hall, winter and spring
15th November	1854	Death of son Hugh Stowell, aged three years
December	1854	Birth of daughter Dora (fifth child)
June	1856	Public lecture about Palmer the poisoner
	1858	Birth of daughter Bertha (sixth child)
12th May	1859	Speaks at opening of Cemetery Road Baptist Church, Sheffield
April/June	1859	Birth of daughter Eleanor (seventh child)
25th September	1859	Chapel reopened after alteration and enlargement
Summer	1860	Open-air summer lectures on Sunday evenings
7th April	1861	Living at 97 Lime Street with Alice and five children
9th April	1861	Preaches at opening of Metropolitan Tabernacle, London
	1861	Founding of the Workman's Bank
	1861	Ends Concert Hall lectures (Lord Nelson Street)

January	1862	Birth of son Frederick Thomson (eighth child)
June	1862	Twenty-two from Laffak, St Helens baptised at Myrtle Street
5th May	1863	Lecture in Luton on 'The Battles of Life'
24th August	1863	Death of wife Alice
June	1865	Marries Phoebe Caine
8th July	1865	Living at 274 Upper Parliament Street
1st December	1866	Death of son Frederick Thomson, aged four years, eleven months
	1867	Solway Street Church opens
	1868	Marriage of Alice Brown (aged nineteen) and William Caine
29th September	1869	Opening of St Helens Church with ninety-five members
	1869	Opening of Stockwell Orphanage, with help from Myrtle St
	1870	F B Meyer settles at Pembroke Chapel, Liverpool, from Oxford
2nd April	1871	Lives at 26 Falkner St with Phoebe and three children
20th July	1871	Charles M Birrell preaches at opening of Toxteth Tabernacle
	1872	F B Meyer leaves Liverpool
15th August	1872	Begins voyage to America
25th August	1872	Preaches in New York

	1872	Travels around Canada and US
28th October	1872	Begins voyage back to Britain
7th November	1872	Returns from America
	1872	Widnes Church opens
January	1873	Twenty-five years of pastorate marked
7th Feb-7th Mar	1875	D L Moody in Liverpool, 128 added to Myrtle Street
	1875	Earlestown Church opens
	1876	Goldborne Street Church, Warrington, opens
June	1876	Period of illness and recuperation in Harrogate
25th November	1876	Speech to the Liverpool Manx Society
	1877	Mill Street church enlarged
29th April	1878	Becomes president of Baptist Union
	1878	Son John marries Mary Neild
May	1878	Juno Street Church opens
19th September	1878	Daughter Dora marries David Taylor in Liverpool
	1878	H F Lapham appointed assistant minister
9th October	1878	Presidential address to Baptist Union autumn session
	1879	Started writing *Notes of My Life*

	1879	Aughton Church placed under Myrtle Street
	1880	Daughter Bertha marries Morton Haig
	1880	H F Lapham resigns
13th August	1880	Tenders resignation from pastorate of Myrtle Street
4th October	1880	Opening of Liverpool House at Stockwell Orphanage
3rd April	1881	Living at 29 Falkner Square with Phoebe and four servants
	1881	Princes Gate Church opened
October	1882	Spurgeon preaches at BU session in Liverpool
25th March	1884	Death of wife Phoebe
	1884	Prescot Church placed under Myrtle Street
	1886	Stops writing *Notes of My Life*
24th February	1886	Death of Hugh Stowell Brown
27th February	1886	Funeral at Everton Necropolis (Low Hill Cemetery)
28th February	1886	am: Eulogy preached at Myrtle St by Dr Alexander Maclaren
		pm: Eulogy preached by Rev Samuel Pearson
	1887	Rev Duncan P McPherson appointed pastor at Myrtle Street

Index

Frodsham, 64
Fuller, Andrew, 69, 141
Fullerite, 69

Gee, William, 92
General Baptists, 128, 161
Gibbons, Joseph, 91
Gibson, Thomas, 94
Gladstone, William, 54, 142,
    150, 183
Glasgow, 68, 194, 200, 222
Glover, Richard, 100
Godfrey, G, 71-72, 76, 87
Golborne Street chapel,
    Warrington, 90
Grand Olympic Festival, 147
Grand Union canal, 39
Grange Road Presbyterian
    Church, 197
Grant Gardens, 191
Grant, Ulysses S, 153, 157
Great Exhibition, 153
Great George Street Chapel, 28,
    59, 80, 195
Greek, 28, 47, 50-51, 194
Greeley, Horace, 153
Grove City Bible Conference,
    201

Haig, Bertha (née Brown), 175,
    184-185, 257, 260
Haig, Morton, 185, 260
Harborne, 37-38, 254
Harris, G, 193
Harrison, Mr, 63
Harrogate, 96, 98, 154, 259
Harwell, Harriet, 176
Hassan, Edward, 193

Heard, John Bickford, 212
Hebrew, 51, 194-195
Helwys, Thomas, 64
Hillary, William, 15-16
Hope Hall, 215
Hope Street, 13-14, 70, 203, 224,
    229, 232-233
Horton Academy, 79
housing, 13, 21, 27, 39, 79, 120-
    121, 201, 204, 237, 240-241,
    251
Howard, Thomas, 25, 61
Hoxton, 107
Huddersfield, 9, 201
Hudson River, 154
Hulley, John, 147-148
Huskisson, William, 226-227
Huss, John (Jan), 130
Hutchinson, Mary, 186
Hutton, William, 197

Illustrated News of the World,
    78, 82, 112
Independent Church, 18, 28-29,
    37, 42, 44, 63, 99
Independent Order of the
    Rechabites, 144
India, 141, 143
Indiana, 148
infant baptism, 25, 29, 51-52
Inman Line, 151
Ireland, 40, 78, 120, 127, 143,
    148, 172, 176, 185
Irish Famine, 78, 120, 143
Isle of Man, 10, 13, 15-16, 18-23,
    31-32, 39, 49-51, 55, 59, 61, 63,
    72-73, 76, 89, 127, 132-133,
    135-136, 144, 174-175, 207

United States, 107, 113, 148, 151-160, 162, 183, 201, 208
University College Liverpool (University of Liverpool), 185
Upper Parliament Street, 87, 186, 221, 258

Vauxhall, 78
Victoria Building (Victoria Gallery), 185-186
voluntarism, voluntaryism, 157-158, 207-208

Wales, 127, 174, 182, 201
Wallasey, 181
Wallington, John, 91
Walton, John, 91
Warrington, 32, 63, 89, 253
Washington DC, 157
Watts, Isaac, 75
Wavertree, 193, 201-202
Wavertree Congregational Church, 193
Weight, George, 46-47
Wellington, 37
Wesley, Charles, 48
Wesley, John, 48, 223
Wesley, Susanna, 48
Wesleyans, 18, 108
Whitchurch, 184
White House, 157
White, Verner M, 80
Widnes, 90, 259
Wirral, 91, 184-185, 202
Wolverhampton, 37
Wolverton, 10, 39-43, 45-49, 56-58, 145, 211, 255

Workman's Bank, 137-141, 168, 221, 223, 257
Worlock, Derek, 233
Wycliffe, John, 130

Yeatman, R, 91
York, 38, 49
Yorkshire, 40, 65-66, 96, 201
Youlen, Alexander, 56
Young, Brigham, 152, 155